Stevenson College Edinburgh.
Library

A26062

WITHDRAWN

KV-179-280

Transport Trends

ISSUES

Volume 119

Series Editor

Craig Donnellan

Assistant Editor

Lisa Firth

STEVENSON COLLEGE LIBRARY		
ACC. No.	WITHDRAWN	
CLASS		388 Don
CAT 18506 AN	PROC CB 25.5.06	

Independence

Educational Publishers
Cambridge

Stevenson College
Bankhead Ave EDIN EH11 4DE

First published by Independence
PO Box 295
Cambridge CB1 3XP
England

© Craig Donnellan 2006

Copyright
This book is sold subject to the condition that it shall not,
by way of trade or otherwise, be lent, resold, hired out or otherwise
circulated in any form of binding or cover other than that in which it
is published without the publisher's prior consent.

Photocopy licence
The material in this book is protected by copyright. However, the
purchaser is free to make multiple copies of particular articles for instructional
purposes for immediate use within the purchasing institution.
Making copies of the entire book is not permitted.

British Library Cataloguing in Publication Data
Transport Trends – (Issues Series)
I. Donnellan, Craig II. Series
388'.0941

ISBN 1 86168 352 9

Printed in Great Britain
MWL Print Group Ltd

Layout by
Lisa Firth

Cover
The illustration on the front cover is by
Don Hatcher.

CONTENTS

Chapter One: Our Transport Problem

Chapter Two: Transport Solutions

Introduction

Transport Trends is the one hundred and nineteenth volume in the **Issues** series. The aim of this series is to offer up-to-date information about important issues in our world.

Transport Trends looks at the problem with transport in Britain today, and at solutions to issues such as pollution and road safety.

The information comes from a wide variety of sources and includes:
Government reports and statistics
Newspaper reports and features
Magazine articles and surveys
Website material
Literature from lobby groups
and charitable organisations.

It is hoped that, as you read about the many aspects of the issues explored in this book, you will critically evaluate the information presented. It is important that you decide whether you are being presented with facts or opinions. Does the writer give a biased or an unbiased report? If an opinion is being expressed, do you agree with the writer?

Transport Trends offers a useful starting-point for those who need convenient access to information about the many issues involved. However, it is only a starting-point. Following each article is a URL to the relevant organisation's website, which you may wish to visit for further information.

*****

Transport trends

Summary of *Transport Trends 2005*, a Department for Transport National Statistics publication

Roads, vehicles and congestion

Road traffic has grown by 81 per cent since 1980, although it has grown less during the 1990s than in the 1980s. Many factors have affected traffic levels, including an increase in car ownership and numbers of drivers, falls in car occupancy levels, fuel price changes and varying levels of capital and current expenditure on roads. Over a quarter of households now have access to two or more cars, more than the proportion of households without access to a car. Men are still more likely to have a driving licence but the proportion of women holding a licence has been increasing at a faster rate.

Personal travel by mode

Car use has continued to increase as disposable income has risen, against a backdrop of little change in the real cost of motoring and rising real costs of public transport fares. While the average time people spend travelling has hardly changed, at around one hour per day, increased car use has allowed them to travel further in the same time.

Public transport

The number of bus journeys has declined from the mid 1980s to the mid 1990s, but has shown some increase over the past 6 years, mainly because of increased bus use in London. Bus operators are now investing in newer vehicles, and passenger satisfaction is generally high although buses tend to have a poorer image among non-users and infrequent users. Rail travel has increased by over 40 per cent over the last 10 years despite the effects of the Hatfield crash in October 2000. Investment in national rail infrastructure has increased significantly since privatisation. The reliability of train services has been improving gradually since 2000, as has passenger satisfaction with journeys undertaken.

Variation in personal travel and access to services

The number of trips made and distance travelled increase with income. Adults in households with two or more cars travel on average over three times further than those in households without a car. On average, men travel a third further than women do. The proportion of people experiencing difficulty getting to medical and shopping facilities has decreased in recent years.

Freight and logistics

The weight of goods lifted in Britain has increased by 25 per cent since 1980 with most of that increase happening during the 1980s. This rise was largely due to increases in the amount of goods lifted by road. Another important freight measure is tonne kilometres moved (defined as tonnes carried multiplied by kilometres travelled). This too has increased, rising 44 per cent since 1980.

Ports and airports

UK residents made 64 million overseas visits in 2004 compared with 18 million in 1980, while the number of visits to the UK by overseas residents increased from 12 million in 1980 to 28 million in 2004. The growth in air travel accounts for the majority of these increases.

Safety

In terms of fatalities per passenger kilometre, air continues to be the safest mode of transport. The passenger fatality rate for cars, the mode of transport used most, has halved since 1980. Vehicle related thefts in England and Wales have halved since they peaked in the mid 1990s.

Health and the environment

Walking and cycling for travel purposes have both declined significantly over the past twenty years. The accompanying growth in motorised transport has resulted in a 47 per cent increase in carbon dioxide emissions from transport sources since 1980, which now account for 23 per cent of UK carbon dioxide emissions. Emissions of local air pollutants have declined with the advent of catalytic converters and cleaner fuels. Despite an improvement in vehicle fuel efficiency, the fuel consumed by transport has increased due to growth in road traffic and a substantial rise in international aviation. The prices of petrol and diesel are roughly the same in real terms as they were in 1980.

■ Information from the Department for Transport. See www.dft.gov.uk

© Crown copyright

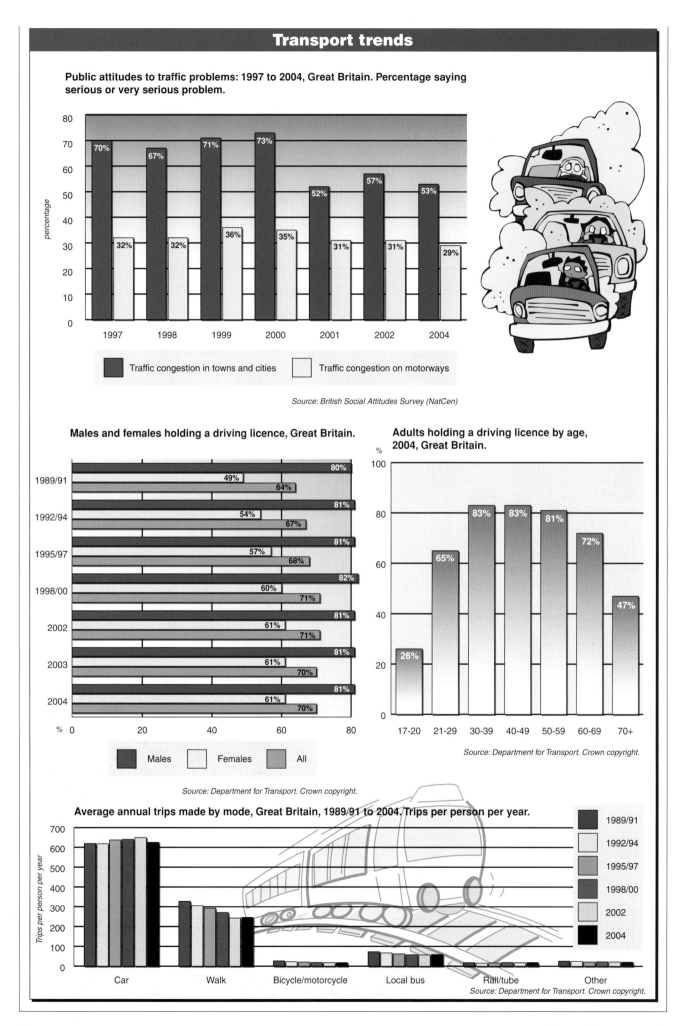

Public attitudes to traffic problems: 1997 to 2004, Great Britain. Percentage saying serious or very serious problem.

Legend:
- Traffic congestion in towns and cities
- Traffic congestion on motorways

1997: 70% / 32%
1998: 67% / 32%
1999: 71% / 36%
2000: 73% / 35%
2001: 52% / 31%
2002: 57% / 31%
2004: 53% / 29%

Source: British Social Attitudes Survey (NatCen)

Males and females holding a driving licence, Great Britain.

Year	Males	Females	All
1989/91	80%	49%	64%
1992/94	81%	54%	67%
1995/97	81%	57%	68%
1998/00	82%	60%	71%
2002	81%	61%	71%
2003	81%	61%	70%
2004	81%	61%	70%

Legend: Males, Females, All

Source: Department for Transport. Crown copyright.

Adults holding a driving licence by age, 2004, Great Britain.

17-20: 26%
21-29: 65%
30-39: 83%
40-49: 83%
50-59: 81%
60-69: 72%
70+: 47%

Source: Department for Transport. Crown copyright.

Average annual trips made by mode, Great Britain, 1989/91 to 2004. Trips per person per year.

Legend: 1989/91, 1992/94, 1995/97, 1998/00, 2002, 2004

Categories: Car, Walk, Bicycle/motorcycle, Local bus, Rail/tube, Other

Source: Department for Transport. Crown copyright.

Vehicle speeds in Great Britain 2004

Information from the Department for Transport

The Department for Transport today published National Statistics of vehicle speeds in Great Britain in 2004. These statistics relate to the speeds at which drivers choose to drive in free-flow conditions generally across the road network. The latest figures show that the proportion of motorists exceeding the speed limit in 2004 changed very little from 2003 although driving in excess of the speed limit remains at a high level on all types of road.

The main features of the new statistics released today are:

On roads with 30 mph limits (built-up)
- On roads with a 30 mph speed limit 53 per cent of cars exceeded that limit compared with 58 per cent in 2003; 25 per cent travelled faster than 35 mph, the same as in 2003.

> **On roads with a 30 mph speed limit 53 per cent of cars exceeded that limit in 2004, compared with 58 per cent in 2003**

- On 30 mph roads, 24 per cent of motorcycles were travelling at more than 35 mph compared with 29 per cent in 2003.
- The survey also reveals a high incidence of speeding by heavy goods vehicles on built-up 30 mph roads: 49 per cent of 2-axle heavy goods vehicles exceeded the speed limit, 18 per cent by more than 5 mph. This is a reduction from the 2003 levels of 53 and 21 per cent respectively.

On roads with 40 mph limits (built-up)
- On 40 mph roads 27 per cent of cars exceeded the limit, with 10 per cent exceeding 45 mph, the same percentages as observed in 2003 and 2002.
- 19 per cent of motorcycles on 40 mph roads were travelling at more than 45 mph. This is the same level as in 2003.

On other roads (non-built-up)
- More than half the cars on motorways and 48 per cent of cars on dual carriageways travelled faster than the speed limit; 19 per cent were travelling faster than 80 mph on motorways, and 14 per cent on dual carriageways.
- The proportion of motorcycles travelling at more than 80 mph on motorways remained at 28 per cent in 2004; whilst on dual carriageways the proportion fell from 23 per cent to 21 per cent.
- On major, non-built-up single carriageway roads, 78 per cent of articulated HGVs were exceeding their 40 mph limit (28 per cent by more than 10 mph). The average speed recorded for articulated HGVs on these roads was 46 mph, just 2 mph less than the average speed of cars (48 mph), for which the limit is 60 mph.

19 May 2005

- The above information is reprinted with kind permission from the Department for Transport. Visit www.dft.gov.uk for more information.

© Crown copyright

15 OVER THE LIMIT? REALLY? MY SPEEDOMETER MUST BE BROKEN!

PATHETIC EXCUSES FOR SPEEDING NO.167

Lowest road deaths

Information from the Department for Transport

The number of people killed on Britain's roads in 2004 was the lowest figure since records began in 1926, figures published by the Department for Transport today show.

In 2004, 3,221 people died in road accidents, down 287 or 8% on the figures from 2003 when 3,508 people were killed. This is despite an estimated increase in road traffic of 2 per cent in 2004.

Road safety Minister Stephen Ladyman said: 'The figures released today are very encouraging, with a substantial drop in the number of people who died on Britain's roads. However, one year's figures should not make anyone feel complacent. Nearly 9 people a day still died in road accidents last year and that figure is still too high.

In 2004, 3,221 people died in road accidents, down 287 or 8% on the figures from 2003

'Britain has one of the best road safety records in the world and the Government is committed to improving it further. We are currently taking a Road Safety Bill through Parliament which contains a raft of measures to build on the progress we are making. The Government will continue to highlight the importance of road safety and to remind all road users of their responsibilities to themselves and others.'

The Government has a target for reducing casualties by 2010. We want to see:
- 40 per cent reduction in the number of people killed or seriously injured in road accidents compared with the average for 1994-98;
- 50 per cent reduction in the number of children killed or seriously injured;
- 10 per cent reduction in the slight casualty rate, expressed as the number of people slightly injured per 100 million vehicle kilometres.

Against these targets, the figures for casualties in 2004 indicate that:
- the number of people killed or seriously injured was 28 per cent below the baseline;
- the number of children killed or seriously injured was 43 per cent below the baseline;
- the provisional estimate of the rate of slight casualties per 100 million vehicle kilometres was 20 per cent below the 1994-98 average.

30 June 2005

- The above information is reprinted with kind permission from the Department for Transport. Visit www.dft.gov.uk for more information.

© Crown copyright

Majority of motorists speed

Information from the Environmental Transport Association

Britain is a nation of speeding motorists with the majority admitting to flouting legal speed limits on motorways and in built-up areas, a new survey claims.

Some 95 per cent of the 2,000 motorists surveyed by *Auto Trader* magazine said they broke the 70mph speed limit on motorways.

Almost three-quarters also admitted speeding in built up areas. And 85 per cent voiced their support for the introduction of variable speed limits.

Speed cameras also came in for criticism with three-quarters of drivers surveyed claiming these prove more of a distraction than a help with four out of five claiming they should only be installed at accident black spots.

The majority also believed that cameras were more of a money-making ploy than a safety measure with a fifth claiming they ignored them completely.

Tony Vickers from the Association of British Drivers said that raising speed limits would mean less tailgating.

He said: '95 per cent of motorists are not irresponsible speed freaks. The speed limit is set too low. It's an anachronism. It was set when the typical car would struggle to reach 70mph.

'Nowadays, ABS, modern tyres, suspension and brakes mean that 90mph is well within the capabilities of most cars in reasonable conditions.'

Paul Smith of the Safe Speed road safety campaign added: 'Drivers know as if by instinct that speed cameras are the wrong safety policy. They have failed to save lives. They have failed to convince the public. They have even failed to stop us speeding.'

But the Department for Transport (DfT) maintained that the cameras are in place to improve road safety, saving 1,750 lives a year.

1 February 2006

- The above information is reprinted with kind permission from the Environmental Transport Association. Visit www.eta.co.uk for more information.

© Adfero Ltd

Child pedestrians

Information from the Child Accident Prevention Trust

How many child pedestrians are killed and injured?

Pedestrian injury is the leading cause of accidental death of children in Great Britain.

In 2003 in Great Britain, among children aged under 16 years,

- 74 pedestrians were killed
- 2,307 pedestrians were seriously injured
- 10,163 pedestrians suffered less severe injuries such cuts and bruises
- In total, 12,544 children were injured as pedestrians.

Five children aged under 16 were killed in Scotland in 2003, 268 were seriously injured and 924 were slightly hurt. (These figures are included in the 'Great Britain' totals shown above.)

In Northern Ireland in 2002, 7 children were killed, 79 were seriously injured and 214 were slightly injured.

The majority of these accidents happen where children spend most time – close to home in residential streets.

There are a number of factors that influence the number of child pedestrian accidents:

Speed

The faster the traffic, the greater the risk of death and serious injury. When children are hit by cars travelling at 20mph five in a hundred are killed, most suffer only minor injuries and about 30 in a hundred suffer no injury at all. At 30mph nearly half of all children are killed and many are seriously injured. At 40mph 85 in every hundred children are killed

Driver behaviour and child development

Children make unpredictable pedestrians. Traffic-coping skills are complex and children do not have the ability to judge speed, distance and danger accurately until around the age of 11. Even children above this age are easily distracted and may not always behave as drivers expect. Young children are also much smaller

child accident prevention trust

than adults and so difficult to see. In residential streets drivers need to compensate by driving slowly enough to be able to stop safely in time for a child.

Economic and social factors

Social and economic factors play a part in child pedestrian injuries. Research has shown that children from social class V are five times more likely to be killed than those from social class I. Children whose families have fewer resources tend to live near more dangerous road environments, have fewer provisions for safe places to play, and tend to go out as pedestrians more often than children from wealthier homes.

Gender

Almost twice as many boys than girls are killed or seriously injured as pedestrians.

How do we compare to other countries in Europe?

The United Kingdom has the one of lowest rates of child road traffic deaths in Europe. However, the UK rates for child pedestrian deaths do not compare as well to the rest of Europe, with Wales and Scotland having particularly high rates. In 2001, the lowest child pedestrian death rate per 100,000 population was in Denmark.

What can be done to reduce child pedestrian accidents?

Central and local government have vital roles to play in the prevention of child pedestrian injuries through the control and regulation of traffic, speed and driver behaviour and the design of safer environments. The

following measures have all been shown to have an effect in reducing pedestrian accidents:

- traffic calming including speed bump and 20mph speed zones
- traffic management that encourages drivers to avoid residential streets
- pedestrian crossings, parking restrictions and the provision of playgrounds all help to make the environment safer for children
- the creation of 'Home Zones' in residential streets where speeds are kept to around 10 mph and pedestrians and cyclists have priority over cars. (Visit http://www.homezonenews.org.uk/).

Road safety education can also play a part in reducing pedestrian casualties:

Children do not have the ability to judge speed, distance and danger accurately until around the age of 11

- drivers need to learn that low speeds in residential areas and around schools and playgrounds will increase their chance of stopping in time and will reduce the likelihood of serious injury and death if they are in collision with a child.
- parents need information to understand their children's ability to cope with traffic and to be able to help their children learn pedestrian skills over time.
- children need adult supervision, roadside pedestrian skills training and road safety education in schools. Many local authorities run pedestrian training schemes in conjunction with schools.
- in Scotland, the Scottish Road Safety Campaign runs the Children's Traffic Club that provides

resources to parents to assist them with road safety education of young children (http://www.road-safety.org.uk/).

- 'walking bus' schemes, which allow children to walk to and from school in supervised groups safely, can help children learn how to negotiate roads safely – again ask your road safety officer about such schemes or visit http://www.saferoutestoschools.org.uk/.

Further information

- The Department for Transport produces pedestrian safety information for children and lesson plans for teachers. See http://www.think.dft.gov.uk/ or http://www.hedgehogs.gov.uk/arrivealive/index.htm for details.
- The Scottish Road Safety Campaign produces a range of programme materials and advice (http://www.road-safety.org.uk/). In Wales, the Road Safety Council of Wales Cyngor Diogelwch y Ffyrdd Cymru coordinates activities (http://www.roscow.org.uk/).
- Contact your road safety officer (at your local council in England and Wales, or via the police in Scotland) for information on local programmes and resources.

- The above information is re-printed with kind permission from the Child Accident Prevention Trust. For information on other child safety topics see CAPT's website at http://www.capt.org.uk

© CAPT

Road safety quiz

How safe are you out on the streets or behind the wheel? Check out your safety knowledge by trying our quiz

1 How many deaths from cycling accidents involve a head injury?
a One-quarter
b Half
c Three-quarters

2 By what percentage can a cycle helmet reduce the risk of a head injury?
a 25%
b 45%
c 85%

3 How many child cyclists wear a cycle helmet?
a One in five
b Two in five
c Three in five

4 At 10 miles per hour over the 30 miles per hour speed limit, how much further does it take a car to stop?
a 15 feet / 4.3 metres / 1 car length
b 30 feet / 8.7 metres / 2 car lengths
c 45 feet / 13 metres / 3 car lengths

5 How many drivers admit to regularly breaking the speed limit in built-up areas?
a Three out of ten
b Five out of ten
c Seven out of ten

6 If hit by a car travelling at 40 miles per hour, how many pedestrians are killed?
a Three in ten
b Six in ten
c Nine in ten

7 How many children injured while crossing a road admit they did not stop before they stepped off the kerb?
a One in nine
b One in six
c One in three

8 Wearing a seat belt and holding a baby on your lap at the same time is safe
a True
b False

9 Up to what age is it recommended that a child uses a booster seat or booster cushion together with their seat belt?
a Five
b Seven
c Eleven

10 It is dangerous to use a rear-facing baby seat in the front seat if the car has a front passenger airbag
a True
b False

Check it, don't chance it! Don't leave safety to chance. Quick, simple checks can prevent many childhood accidents. For more information on keeping children safe, visit Child Accident Prevention Trust's website at www.capt.org.uk.

ANSWERS
Q1: c Q2: c Q3: a Q4: c Q5: c Q 6: c Q7: c Q8: b Q 9: c Q10: a

© CAPT

RAC report on motoring 2005

A summary

Car dependency is now at its highest level since RAC began monitoring it 17 years ago. Now nine in 10 motorists would find it very difficult to adjust their lifestyles to being without a car and admit to using their car every single day. With the average motorist clocking up nearly 11,000 miles per year and almost half of them being part of a two-,;.lcar family, it's clear that the car has a pivotal role in British life. But with this dependency and in order to retain an individual's 'right to drive' comes a trade-off; owning and using a car is often far from being fun and enjoyable. It comes with various frustrations and some considerable dangers, which if we are to attempt to mitigate, need to be tackled in a concerted way. This Report focuses on how we might do that in order to bring more enjoyment back to driving.

The majority of British motorists are underwhelmed by car ownership, considering their vehicle to be 'just another household appliance' which they are increasingly dependent upon in daily life. Smaller proportions confess to a more emotional bond, with 22% considering their car to be

'a toy to have some fun with', 24% as 'something impressive to be seen in' and 29% 'a close friend or confidante'. Not surprisingly, it is the younger, 'flashier' drivers who are most likely to consider their cars in one of these ways; older and low mileage drivers are far more ambivalent. With this in mind, it figures that many motorists think driving is a drag; 44% of them believe that 'All the fun has gone out of driving these days' and only 14% disagree strongly with this sentiment. Again, it is younger drivers who find motoring most fun (perhaps because passing their test represents a taste of real freedom and adulthood), a factor that diminishes slightly the more points one gains on one's licence for driving offences.

Our sample was not uniform in identifying the types of thing that make driving tough or irritating; when offered the choice of 10 factors that would make driving

more enjoyable the vote was split. However, the top three choices were: making middle and fast lane hogging a driving offence, removing speed bumps and removing all speed cameras. These choices point to a reality on our roads: drivers are individuals and in most cases consider their motoring experiences selfishly rather than with the good of all road users in mind. These results also suggest that other motorists' selfish behaviour is most annoying to them, followed closely by initiatives that place restrictions on their own driving speed.

With the average motorist clocking up nearly 11,000 miles per year and almost half of them being part of a two-car family, it's clear that the car has a pivotal role in British life

---

But it is looking at the entirety of the picture rather than individual behaviours that allows us to understand some of the problems, frustrations and agonies that motorists face. Though congestion and selfish driving may be annoying they are nowhere near as critical as tackling the problems that result in nearly 300,000 deaths and serious injuries on our roads every year, a good proportion of which are caused by speeding or drink driving, and increasingly other offences of dangerous driving.

In order to understand how and why some drivers commit these types of dangerous offences, we need to understand the main traits that

STUPID DRIVER!!!

make drivers tick. The RAC *Report on Motoring* has identified seven key traits that are present to different degrees in each driver. The Report then describes six major typologies which make up the vast majority of British motorists, demonstrating that though some of them pose few significant road safety risks, others are far more inclined to drive dangerously, recklessly and to habitually break motoring laws. The two worst offending groups are made up of young and middle-aged male drivers who either see driving as a game or as necessity where it's easy to transgress the law and not get caught if you're clever about it. By reaching these motorists and seeking to change their behaviours we might improve this country's road safety record, whilst at the same time improving standards amongst other motorists, many of whom admit to frequent minor infringements.

Although 84% of our sample considered themselves to be law-abiding, 55% admit to exceeding the speed limit a little every day

---

Although 84% of our sample considered themselves to be law-abiding, 55% admit to exceeding the speed limit a little every day. Compared to last year's Report, we have seen a significant increase in the admission of lawless behaviour, with speeding being the most common offence. This has come at the same time as record numbers of speeding convictions that have been made by police and Safety Camera Partnerships suggesting that detection has improved. Public awareness campaigns have sought to demonstrate the fact that dangerous and inappropriate speeding kills. The defiant admission of speeding behaviour by our sample has also corresponded with some anger about the use of cameras for speed policing. Few motorists consider that the current regime

Distance travelled by region

Average distance travelled by mode of travel by region of residence – GO Region and Country: 2003/04.[1] Miles per person per year.

	Walk[2]	Car driver	Car passenger	Other private	Local bus	Other public	All modes
North East	199	2,798	1,689	198	352	563	5,799
North West	198	3,230	1,832	194	226	457	6,137
Yorkshire/Humber	183	3,277	1,999	218	258	419	6,355
East Midlands	206	4,070	2,258	332	193	383	7,443
West Midlands	179	3,636	2,010	172	273	468	6,737
East	178	4,074	2,396	262	148	732	7,791
London	211	1,792	1,254	156	456	1,179	5,048
South East	204	4,198	2,213	249	145	708	7,716
South West	194	4,313	2,472	253	190	497	7,919
England	195	3,487	2,007	223	245	629	6,787
Wales	158	3,694	2,109	355	240	338	6,895
Scotland	199	3,172	2,125	197	398	759	6,850
Great Britain	*194*	*3,467*	*2,023*	*227*	*260*	*628*	*6,798*

1. Combined survey years 2003 and 2004
2. Short walks are believed to be under-recorded in 2002-2003 compared with other years.

Source: National Travel Survey. Crown copyright.

will make them slow down or stick to the speed limit as a matter of course; our more fervent speeders would respond to more traffic Police or a 'big brother' system where their movements are monitored by an in-car electronic device. A mixture of human detection and high-tech monitoring could be used to clamp down on dangerous speeders. If increased penalties were introduced to attempt to deter perpetual and dangerous speeders, schemes would have to be rather draconian to effect a major behavioural change, for example, instant driving bans or prison sentences. As these penalties seem unrealistic and politically unacceptable it may be that improved enforcement and detection would be the most appropriate means with which to experiment, together with education schemes, such as driver retraining and speed awareness. At

the same time, motorist goodwill could be fostered by donating the balance of revenue relating to fines to a road safety fund rather than it going to the Treasury. Finally, given that the Report suggests that the worst offenders might be 'named and shamed' into better behaviour, a requirement for displaying their penalty points on their windscreen might lead to an improvement in behaviour.

Drink and drug driving remain considerable problems for law enforcers and policy makers to address. Amongst some, particularly younger age groups, this behaviour is on the increase so concerted action needs to be taken to halt this worrying trend. 20% of the sample admitted to drink driving, with by far the highest incidence coming amongst young, male drivers in London. Given the fact that drink driving is largely socially unacceptable and hard-hitting education campaigns have been in existence now for many years, it's perhaps unsurprising that perpetual drink drivers would only change their behaviour if a technical solution, like an alcolock, was to prevent their car starting or if they felt the real likelihood of being caught was far greater than it currently is. Therefore, serious focus should go into the development of alcolock devices; fitting them as standard in passenger vehicles could certainly be a cheaper solution than the enforcement resources that might be necessary to make motorists believe that they have a good chance of being stopped on any journey. Only very severe penalty regimes such as lifetime or long-term driving bans would have the same impact on behaviour as the alcolock, though there could be a role for 'naming and shaming' offenders or reducing the current legal alcohol limit. Better roadside detection methods would certainly help crack down on the worrying increase in drug driving, whilst continued education is essential to communicate the dangers of both drink and drug driving.

Interestingly, though motorists consider transgressions like driving with a hand-held mobile phone to be dangerous if committed by other drivers, many consider their own driving skills to be beyond reproach

---

Beyond the sphere of the most dangerous driving habits are a number of anti-social traits, some of which can and do lead to accidents. Interestingly, though motorists consider transgressions like driving with a hand-held mobile phone to be dangerous if committed by other drivers, many consider their own driving skills to be beyond reproach; 76% believe themselves to be safer than other drivers. These attitudes are perhaps symptomatic of today's 'me' society. This said, worrying numbers of motorists admit to a range of poor and dangerous habits ranging from jumping red lights, undertaking and blocking junctions to road rage, using a hand-held mobile and cutting people up. Few consider this behaviour to be serious or dangerous, particularly as they rarely get caught. Yet again, it would take a radical increase in detection and more

stringent penalties for this sort of behaviour to change. An enhanced commitment to highly visible road policing, announced by the Transport Minister, the Home Office and the Association of Chief Police Officers in January 2005, is an important step towards providing an active deterrent. Education also has a part to play to remind the worst offenders what's legal and the impact of their discourteous and often dangerous behaviour.

Illegal parking is rarely dangerous to other road users but it is a source of frustration for motorists, many of whom believe that there are too few legal spaces available and far too stringent and draconian an enforcement regime. RAC believes that this source of motorist agony has received enough penalty and enforcement focus and that more attention should now be paid to more serious transgressions, such as a failure by large numbers of motorists to keep their vehicle documentation up to date. Those guilty of this are creating a growing motoring 'underclass' whose actions often cost law-abiding motorists dearly as a result of collisions with uninsured or unroadworthy vehicles. Whilst this behaviour certainly needs to be dealt with in the most concerted fashion,

a considerable number (11%) of usually law-abiding motorists do admit to some dishonesty when it comes to gaining an insurance quote by lying about where the car is parked overnight. Could it be that the cost of certain motoring-related charges is just too much for drivers facing increasing numbers of parking and speeding fines and rising fuel costs?

The Report demonstrates the wide range of issues facing drivers, Government and law enforcers when it comes to dealing with the often hectic and challenging reality that is our British road network. Our hope is that some of the insights it gives into motorists' instincts will help policy makers as they develop strategies of penalty, detection and education and explore preventative measures, particularly those available through in-car technology, to reduce the incidence of bad and dangerous behaviour and make our roads a more enjoyable environment for all to use.

The RAC *Report on Motoring 2005* costs £250.00.

■ The above information is reprinted with kind permission from the RAC. Visit www.rac.co.uk for more information.

© 2005 RAC Motoring Services

Trips made by region

Trips by main mode of travel by region of residence – GO Region and Country: 2003/2004.[1] Trips per person per year.

	Walk[2]	Car driver	Car passenger	Other private	Local bus	Other public	All modes
North East	277	360	213	21	83	29	983
North West	251	411	232	23	60	27	1,004
Yorkshire/Humber	245	379	220	23	60	21	950
East Midlands	265	444	237	32	43	15	1,037
West Midlands	240	434	241	18	65	20	1,019
East	210	438	253	37	31	27	997
London	233	237	153	22	118	95	858
South East	249	460	242	32	31	30	1,044
South West	268	455	255	32	33	13	1,056
England	246	401	227	27	58	33	992
Wales	208	429	237	20	47	20	961
Scotland	256	375	215	20	79	28	972
Great Britain	*245*	*400*	*226*	*26*	*59*	*32*	*989*

1. Combined survey years 2003 and 2004

2. Short walks are believed to be under-recorded in 2002-2003 compared with other years.

Source: National Travel Survey. Crown copyright.

YouGov questioned 2136 adults aged 18+ throughout Britain online between 11th and 13th January 2005. The results have been weighted to the profile of all adults.

Which of these do you use on a normal day's travel to work?

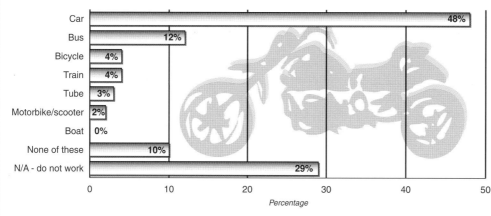

Transport	Percentage
Car	48%
Bus	12%
Bicycle	4%
Train	4%
Tube	3%
Motorbike/scooter	2%
Boat	0%
None of these	10%
N/A - do not work	29%

Percentage

What is your biggest concern about the railways?

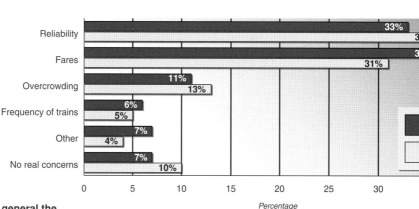

Concern	Male	Female
Reliability	33%	36%
Fares	36%	31%
Overcrowding	11%	13%
Frequency of trains	6%	5%
Other	7%	4%
No real concerns	7%	10%

Percentage

Do you think in general the transport situation in Britain is going to get better, worse or stay the same over the next five years?

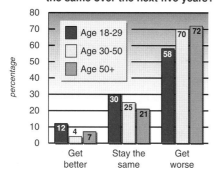

	Age 18-29	Age 30-50	Age 50+
Get better	12	4	7
Stay the same	30	25	21
Get worse	58	70	72

How important is transport in determining your vote at the next election?

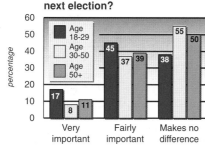

	Age 18-29	Age 30-50	Age 50+
Very important	17	8	11
Fairly important	45	37	39
Makes no difference	38	55	50

If there is an increase in overcrowding and fare increases would that cause you to switch votes at the next election?

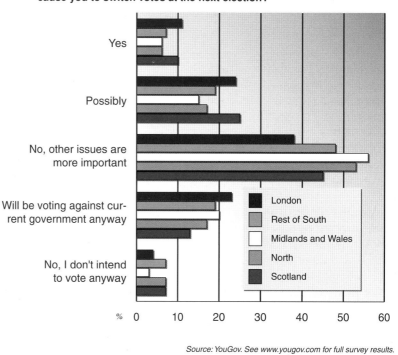

London, Rest of South, Midlands and Wales, North, Scotland

- Yes
- Possibly
- No, other issues are more important
- Will be voting against current government anyway
- No, I don't intend to vote anyway

Source: YouGov. See www.yougov.com for full survey results.

DfT: Britain heading for gridlock

Information from the Environmental Transport Association

Brits have become increasingly dependent on their cars in all aspects of their daily life, a new government report claims.

The study, *Transport Trends*, from the Department for Transport (DfT) says that congestion levels are rising dramatically and that introducing tolls will do too little too late to prevent Britain's roads from becoming gridlocked.

The number of private cars has more than doubled to 26 million over the course of the last 25 years with people now clocking 247 billion miles a year on the road.

Statistics reveal that the average person now spends some 221 hours a year behind the wheel, covering around 5,500 at an average speed of 25mph.

The number of cars on the roads is growing by more than half a million a year

---

Almost two-thirds of shopping trips were made by car last year, compared to half in 1991 as out-of-town retail centres grow in popularity. The number of primary school children being driven to school has risen from 27 per cent to 41 per cent.

More homes now have two cars than no cars at all with five per cent owning at least three vehicles. Almost two-thirds of cars on the road carry only the driver whilst a quarter of all car journeys made last year were under two miles in length.

The increase in car trips caused the amount of walking and cycling to fall to record levels. Last year the average person managed 192 miles compared to 237 miles in 1990.

The number of cars on the roads is growing by more than half a million a year, forcing the government to re-evaluate its targets for cutting congestion levels. Instead of reducing the overall traffic volume by six per cent by 2010, it is now predicting a rise of 20 per cent in car ownership.
3 February 2006

■ Information from the Environmental Transport Association. Visit www.eta.co.uk for more.
© *Adfero Ltd*

Road traffic

Eightfold increase since 1952

Motor vehicles travelled 499 billion kilometres in total on Great Britain's roads in 2004. This was eight times more than in 1952. There was almost continuous growth until 1973. Since then the trend has continued upward, but annual changes have been more erratic.

Just under 80 per cent of road traffic distance, including pedal cycles, was accounted for by cars and taxis in 2004. This compares with less than 40 per cent in 1952.

The number of licensed vehicles in Great Britain has also increased. In 1961 there were fewer than 9 million licensed vehicles. By 1981 there were 19.3 million, and by 2004, 32.3 million. Private cars accounted for an increasing proportion of this total, 59 per cent in 1961, 77 per cent in 1981, and 80 per cent in 2004.

The overall length of Great Britain's road network increased more slowly. Between 1962 and 2004 it grew by around a quarter to 387,700 kilometres.

The increase in the number of motor vehicles, and the greater distances travelled by individuals, has led to large increases in the average daily flow of motor vehicles. Between 1980 and 1990 average traffic flows rose by 43 per cent. Growth slowed in the 1990s, but daily traffic flows still increased by 17 per cent in the ten years to 2004.
10 October 2005

© *Source: Department for Transport. Crown copyright*

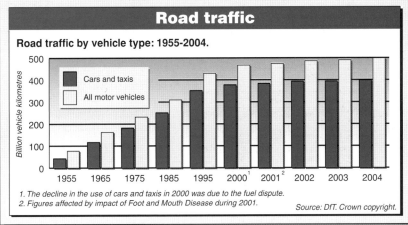

Road traffic

Road traffic by vehicle type: 1955-2004.

Billion vehicle kilometres — legend: Cars and taxis; All motor vehicles

1. The decline in the use of cars and taxis in 2000 was due to the fuel dispute.
2. Figures affected by impact of Foot and Mouth Disease during 2001.

Source: DfT. Crown copyright.

Transport: frequent questions

Information from Global Action Plan

1. If traffic's so bad, why don't we build more roads?

It's really not that simple. Research consistently shows that building more roads doesn't ease traffic – in fact it usually generates more. There is also growing opposition to new road schemes as people become more and more aware of the health and pollution implications.

Naturally there is also the environmental impact to consider. Many UK roads have been built through areas valuable for wildlife, recreation, or their natural beauty – Twyford Down and Newbury, for example. It's no surprise that so many people now believe that enough is enough.

2. Isn't public transport really expensive and unreliable?

Of course we would like to see public transport improved. But even so, in many cases it is still quicker and cheaper than using a car.

If you take long journeys, rail discounts and bargain fares are available if you are able to plan ahead. And for shorter journeys, the cost of petrol and parking can add up to far more than a bus ticket – not to mention the time it takes to find that elusive parking space!

3. Do I have to give up my car?

Not necessarily – everyone can recognise the benefits of cars and for some people they are indispensable. If you do need to use a car, make sure it's as efficiently run as possible.

4. Don't buses cause more pollution than cars?

No they don't. A bus carrying, approximately 20 people will create far less pollution than 20 cars carrying one person each. Buses and coaches, like other vehicles, are now being subjected to stringent random emissions testing in the UK.

5. How succesful are Congestion Charge schemes?

London's congestion charge is £5 for people driving throughout an eight-square-mile zone of central London. Traffic delays inside the charging zone remain 30% lower than before charging was introduced, and bus passenger journeys are up. Other cities, like Edinburgh, are planning to introduce similar schemes.

■ The above information is reprinted with kind permission from Global Action Plan. Visit www. globalactionplan.org.uk for more information.

© Global Action Plan

Rising petrol prices

2005 petrol price rises left £200 hole in family budgets

Petrol price rises throughout 2005 left British families having to compensate for a £200 hole in their budgets across the year, says the AA Motoring Trust. The average price of petrol for December was 87.7 pence per litre, more than eight pence higher than where it began the year.

At its peak in September, when the average price of petrol was 15.2 pence above the January starting level of 79.6 pence per litre, UK households with two car-owning adults were paying on average £33.39 per month more for their petrol. On 14 September the price reached an all-time high of 96.06 pence per litre.

For many families, the overall drain on their yearly funds has dwarfed the combined rise in other domestic and motoring bills:

■ council tax on average up £47 for a Band D property
■ provisional 2005 figures show a £25 increase in the average electricity bill
■ provisional 2005 figures show a £50 increase in the average gas bill
■ average water bills up by £29 in April 2005
■ average comprehensive car insurance premiums rose £9.64
■ average home buildings and contents insurance premiums fell by £3.48 and £0.01 respectively

The same households paid more in road fuel duty and VAT, between 64.6 and 74.1 per cent of the price of a litre of petrol, than in council tax. Whereas the average council tax for a Band D home was £1,214 in 2005, two adult drivers in the household paid on average £1,584 to the Chancellor in petrol taxes.

'This year has been the first since the fuel crisis of the 1970s that the effect of rising car fuel costs has literally hit home,' says Ruth Bridger, petrol price analyst for the AA Motoring Trust. 'The impact on inflation, high-street spending and other commercial activity as consumers cut back in other areas of family expenditure to compensate contributed to a general downturn in business.

'The cost of buying and maintaining a car may have dropped but many families separate those "capital" costs from their weekly budget. They react to what is left in their purses and wallets after they have filled up at the petrol station by trimming their expenditure elsewhere.'

Bridger adds: 'The idea that motorists could be forced to leave their cars at home by raising the price of petrol has been proven wrong, even with prices way above levels anyone imagined. Families still have to go to work, take the children to school, go shopping and all the other trips they need to do.

'However, with the price of petrol unlikely to dip back below 80 pence per litre again and volatile crude oil markets sensitive to any hint of interruption to stretched supply and refining, families are going to have to bend somewhat to new realities.

Wising up to cleverer driving techniques and a smarter choice of car will allow the family budgets to stretch further than they did this summer.'

29 December 2005

■ The above information is reprinted with kind permission from the AA Motoring Trust. For more information, please visit www.aatrust.com

© *The AA Motoring Trust*

The real price of petrol

A school briefing from Transport 2000

Introduction

Anyone who reads the newspapers on a regular basis could be forgiven for thinking that the car-driving population of Britain is being victimised by a hostile government, greedy oil companies and unpredictable oil-producing countries. Petrol prices do yo-yo to some extent, particularly when there is instability in the international oil market, but the overall impression given by motoring organisations and some newspapers is that motoring costs are more generally becoming crippling. Motoring organisations and haulage interests continually call for government duty on petrol and diesel to be reduced to reduce the cost of fuel for cars and lorries.

In this briefing, Transport 2000 sets out some of the facts behind the price of petrol and diesel, motoring costs overall and how we use our cars. It explains just what would happen if motoring became cheaper through lower fuel costs.

Traffic and how we travel

Road traffic grew by 73 per cent between 1980 and 2002. The majority of the growth was in car traffic. Traffic is continuing to rise by between 1 and 2 per cent per year.

Reducing the price of petrol would encourage people to use their cars more and lead to a faster growth in traffic and greater congestion. Already the UK has the most extensive traffic congestion in Europe. Cheaper petrol does not encourage people to buy more fuel-efficient cars, nor to consider whether they really need to drive for a particular trip or could use other transport methods.

People in the UK make more use of cars than any other European country despite having below-average car ownership. The UK has the most extensive traffic congestion in Europe but public transport fares are more expensive than in other European countries, with the exception of Denmark and Sweden.

A quarter of all car trips in 1999/2001 were less than 2 miles in length, ideal for walking or cycling. Cars were used for 18 per cent of trips under 1 mile and for 61 per cent of trips of between 1 and 2 miles. Walking and cycling have both declined significantly over the past 20 years. The distance people walk on average has fallen by about one-third and distance cycled by about 14 per cent.

Twenty-six per cent of households in Britain don't have access to a car. People in low income groups make the fewest car trips. On average, people living in households in the lowest income group made 338 car trips a year (42 per cent of all trips) in 1999/2001 in Britain, compared with a general population average of 639 trips (63 per cent of all trips). People living in households in the highest income group recorded the highest use of cars, 835 trips a year (72 per cent of all trips).

Pollution

Cheaper petrol and diesel would also lead to more pollution. Car exhausts pump a range of pollutants into the atmosphere that are responsible for up to 24,000 premature deaths each year through respiratory and other diseases. Although catalytic converters are making cars cleaner, the continuing rise in traffic is counteracting this.

There was a doubling of asthma cases in children under five during the 1990s. One in eight children now suffer from the condition in the UK, a total of 1.4 million (this figure has increased sixfold over the past 25 years). Eighty-one per cent of people with asthma say that air pollution brings on asthma symptoms. New research shows that pollution can cause asthma in children in the first place, supporting recent evidence from the US that has proved car fumes cause asthma.

Air pollution, including particulates from traffic fumes, could be responsible for one in six cot deaths caused by Sudden Infant Death Syndrome. Air pollution could also be responsible for nearly a quarter of all respiratory disease deaths of normal birth-weight babies under one year old.

Climate change

Carbon dioxide from the transport sector is a growing contributor to climate change. Extreme weather may become more common making life more difficult for all of us. The effects of climate change are not completely understood but other possible results could include drying out of grain-producing areas, growth of deserts and a failure of ocean currents that at the moment bring a mild climate to the UK, possibly leading to much harsher winters. Direct financial losses from climate change could run globally at £213 billion a year by 2050, not counting social and environmental costs. Globally scientists say we need to cut greenhouse gas emissions by 60 per cent by 2050 if we are to avoid catastrophic climate change.

The 73 per cent increase in road traffic between 1980 and 2002 has resulted in a 39 per cent increase in greenhouse gas emissions from transport, which now accounts for 26 per cent of UK emissions. Road transport makes up around 21 per cent of total man-made carbon dioxide emissions in the UK. Carbon dioxide emissions from vehicles in Europe are set to continue rising.

Cars are a very inefficient way of getting around in terms of the fossil fuels burned in the process. The average carbon dioxide emissions for different modes of transport are as follows (in g carbon dioxide per passenger kilometre): passenger rail 73, cars 114, buses 77, short haul air 330.

Fuel tax and the cost of motoring

Over the past 20 years the overall cost of motoring has in real terms, i.e. once inflation is accounted for, remained at or below the 1980 level while bus fares have risen by 31 per cent and rail fares by 37 per cent. The real cost of motoring fell by 4.8 per cent between 1997 and 2003 but during the same period the cost of travelling by train rose by 3 per cent and the cost of travelling by bus rose by 8.2 per cent. Fuel duty is higher in the UK than most other EU countries but the full basket of motoring taxes, including fuel duty, purchase tax, Vehicle Excise Duty (the tax disk) and road tolls, is about average.

Tax on fuel is a general revenue raiser for all governments. It contributes to the whole range of government spending, including education, health care, social security, the police and so on. If fuel duty were to be reduced to satisfy car drivers, it would mean less funding being available for these crucial public services.

The 73 per cent increase in road traffic between 1980 and 2002 has resulted in a 39 per cent increase in greenhouse gas emissions from transport

Motorists don't pay the full cost of their effects on the environment and the community. The external costs of motoring, as they are known, including congestion, road maintenance, air pollution, road crashes, noise and climate change, average 21p/mile, rising to £1/mile in London.

High fuel prices are not popular with rural motorists, who often feel they have no option but to drive. But this is masking the real problem in the countryside: rural communities are increasingly being deprived of even basic facilities because life is based more and more around car travel. Grocery stores, banks, post offices and even schools are being closed across the countryside, while at the same time public transport services are being withdrawn. And so rural people are being forced to drive even further…

Further information

- *Cutting Your Car Use* by Anna Semlyen. This practical guide to help people reduce their car use is published by Green Books, Foxhole, Dartington, Totnes, Devon TQ9 6EB at £3.95 (post free when you mention Transport 2000).

- *The Car Buyers' Guide*. This is an annual guide to the most environmentally friendly cars on sale. Detailed tables compare makes and models on engine size, fuel consumption, speed, noise and emissions to provide a 'best buy' recommendation. This is available from the Environmental Transport Association at 68 High Street, Weybridge, Surrey KT13 8RS or on 0800 212 810 for £5 including postage. Alternatively you can download it from www.eta.co.uk.

- The above information is reprinted with kind permission from Transport 2000. Visit www.transport2000.org.uk for more information.

© Transport 2000

Emissions – what goes in must come out

Cars emit a complex chemical cocktail of exhaust gases. Below is a list of the major pollutants and the damage they are causing to our bodies and our planet

Benzene

The common replacement for lead in petrol is benzene, which is a carcinogenic substance occurring naturally in crude oil. All petrol contains some benzene, but increased use of this dangerous additive could also carry severe penalties for human health.

Carbon dioxide (CO_2)

Although CO_2 is not a health-damaging gas, it is the main cause of climate change and arguably the single biggest pollution threat that humankind faces today.

Road transport is the fastest growing source of CO_2 and accounts for around 25% of Britain's emissions

---

Did you know that 6,000 miles in a car produces roughly its own weight in CO_2? Road transport is the fastest growing source of CO_2 and accounts for around 25% of Britain's emissions. The main way to cut emissions is to reduce our use of fuel, by using more fuel-efficient vehicles and driving less. You can also help offset the emissions you create by making your driving carbon neutral. Call the ETA on 0800 212 810 for more details.

Carbon monoxide (CO)

In Britain, road traffic is responsible for over 70% of CO emissions. CO reduces the oxygen-carrying capacity of the blood and affects the brain's ability to function correctly. It can cause headaches, fatigue and at very high levels, death. There are estimated to be 2/3 of a million unborn babies at risk from the increase in CO in their mothers' blood. CO also adds to ground level ozone, combining with other pollutants to form photochemical smog, and is one of the minor anthropogenic gases causing climate change.

Hydrocarbons (HCs)

These are compounds made of hydrogen and carbon which contribute to summer smog, and can cause throat and eye irritation. Benzene is emitted from both petrol and diesel vehicles and is known to cause cancer. HCs also contribute to global warming.

Nitrogen oxides (NOx)

NOx are the pollutants most strongly linked with acid rain, combining with water vapour to form a dilute but deadly nitric acid solution, causing serious damage and inhibiting the growth of plants. NOx are also contributing pollutants to photochemical smog, they irritate the lungs, and increase susceptibility to viral infections. In Britain, 44% of NOx emissions come from road vehicles.

Particulates

Diesel engines emit particulates (or soot) which is increasingly being linked with asthma. The car makers have been attempting to make the soot particulates smaller – indeed the law requires soot particulates to be of an ever smaller size. However, these micro particulates now penetrate even further into the lungs resulting in less obvious, but longer-term damage. This especially affects children as they utilise their lungs more than adults, their lungs are more susceptible and they are closer to the source of the exhaust fumes. The black, smoky exhaust of a badly maintained diesel vehicle contains dangerously high levels of soot and should be reported to the Smoky Vehicle hotline on 020 8665 0885.

Sulphur dioxide (SO_2)

Petrol and diesel engines also emit small quantities of SO_2 which, in high concentrations, can cause breathing problems, affect plant growth, contribute to acid rain, and damage buildings.

■ Information from the ETA. Visit www.eta.co.uk for more.
© *Environmental Transport Association*

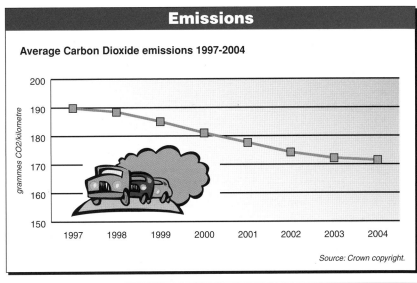

Emissions

Average Carbon Dioxide emissions 1997-2004

grammes CO2/kilometre

Source: Crown copyright.

r pollution from aviation

combustion in aircraft engines is efficient and jet exhausts are almost smoke free, however pollutant emissions from aircraft at ground level are increasing with airport movements. As pollutants from aircraft are emitted at high altitudes where they take longer to disperse, they have a significant impact on the global pollution problems of ozone depletion and global warming. A large amount of air pollution around airports is also generated by surface traffic.

Nitrogen oxides

Nitrogen oxides from aircraft destroy ozone in the upper atmosphere (stratospheric ozone or the ozone layer), damaging the protective layer that filters out harmful radiation from the sun. In the lower atmosphere (troposphere) it contributes to the production of ozone, which in the troposphere is a pollutant and contributes to global warming.

Carbon dioxide

Aircraft currently contribute 3.5% of global carbon dioxide emissions from human acitivities – and this is expected to increase to up to 15% within 50 years, making aviation a major contributor to global warming.

Water vapour

Aircraft vapour trails or contrails can lead to the formation of cirrus clouds. Both vapour trails and clouds have a warming effect, trapping heat on the earth's surface.

Controls

There are no controls on emissions from aircraft. The fact absence of tax on aviation fuel means air travel is relatively cheap. Fuel makes up only 15% of the cost of flying so there is little incentive for airlines to invest in more efficient aircraft. Airlines could be made to contribute to the cost by fuel tax or by paying a levy on emissions. These measures would:

- Ensure airlines pay for the pollution they cause, like other transport operators

- Encourage the development of more fuel-efficient aircraft
- Help reduce the demand for air travel as other options become more competitive
- Be consistent with UK pledges to reduce greenhouse gas emissions pollution from airport operations.

Planning development to meet the projected increased demand in passenger air traffic is also a cause for concern. For example, a study at Gatwick predicted that NOx emissions from cars could decrease due to cleaner vehicles, but emissions from aircraft are expected to double by 2008. This would result in the National Air Quality Standard for NO_2 being exceeded in nearby towns.

Increasing capacity in more rural areas will lead to the erosion of tranquillity, loss of habitats for wildlife and increased surface traffic.

- Information from NSCA, the environmental protection charity. Visit www.nsca.org.uk for more.

© NSCA

Transport facts

Noise, smelly fumes, frustrating traffic jams, road works and stress – just your average car journey. But there is more at stake than uncomfortable travelling: transport is responsible for 25% of the UK's greenhouse gas emissions; small particles emitted by vehicles using petrol or diesel are linked to asthma, and nitrogen oxides cause respiratory diseases and can produce smog at ground level.

Stand beside a busy road on a hot day and you'll smell the odour of this pollutant cocktail. There have been advances in clean technologies like catalytic converters but the benefits of these have been balanced out by the growth in traffic volumes.

Traffic makes a huge amount of noise. Although we've all grown used to living with it imagine what a city would be like with quiet vehicles and streets. It's no coincidence that many more sustainable vehicles are less noisy too.

Facts

1 Air pollution causes between 12,000 and 24,000 early deaths every year.

2 Road traffic is expected to increase by 50% by 2026.

3 In 2001 the total distance travelled by UK vehicles was 474 billion km. That's the equivalent of 40 return trips to the planet Pluto.

4 The average person in the UK drives their car 5,433 miles per year, takes the bus for 207 miles per year and uses the train for 325 miles per year.

5 Bicycle use has been falling steadily since the 1970s, despite the fact that more of us than ever own bicycles.

6 One return flight from London to New York will generate the same amount of CO_2 as driving a family car for 4 months.

7 Bus services in the UK receive less Government subsidy than in any other country in the EU.

8 In the UK, an average car produces approximately 3.3 tonnes of carbon dioxide per year.

9 In many towns and cities, air pollution is often in excess of international standards.

- The above information is reprinted with kind permission from Global Action Plan. Visit www.globalactionplan.org.uk for more information.

© Global Action Plan

'Invisible' speed cameras that track drivers for miles

A new generation of speed cameras that track drivers over long distances is being installed across Britain.

The devices calculate a car's average speed between two points which may be miles apart, unlike existing cameras which can measure speed only at a single point.

The new cameras, called Specs, are also harder for drivers to spot than the familiar yellow boxes.

They are fixed to slim poles above a driver's line of vision and do not flash.

A new generation of speed cameras that track drivers over long distances is being installed across Britain

---

Critics warn that the 'Big Brother' system will be another cash-raising tool designed to persecute drivers.

Those in favour of the new cameras deny they are money-makers, claiming they encourage people to drive at a sensible speed over long distances.

But they catch a high number of drivers. A pair recently introduced in Central London clocked up more than £84,000 in fines in just three weeks. Another pair covering a mile-long stretch of the A610 in Nottinghamshire generate £1million a year.

The new cameras work out a driver's average speed between two sites by capturing the car's registration number at the start and the end of the stretch.

Cars whose average speed is above the limit have their image and registration number retained so that a fixed penalty notice can be sent out automatically.

Specs do not need film because they take electronic or digital images.

About 75 pairs are said to be in operation already but experts predict more will be used around Britain.

They are due to be installed on the A14 in Cambridgeshire as well as on a 28-mile stretch of road on one of Scotland's most dangerous routes, the A77. Nigel Humphries, of the Association of British Drivers, said: 'Drivers will be caught without even knowing it. This is about raising revenue.'

The RAC Foundation has also criticised Specs cameras, saying they are more effective at generating money than cutting speeds.

The Foundation's Edmund King said: 'The problem with them is drivers do not know they are there so they do not deter people from speeding or get them to slow down.'

The amount paid by motorists in speed camera fines soared to more than £112million last year – nearly twice as much as the previous year.

The revelation comes just weeks after it emerged a huge network of hi-tech traffic cameras is to be set up to catch uninsured and untaxed drivers.

The system will be able to read number plates, scan national databases in seconds and warn patrol cars waiting further down the road.

■ This article first appeared in the *Daily Mail*, 4 April 2005.
© 2006 Associated Newspapers Ltd

Limiting speed

Speed of cars 'will be limited by computer'. By David Millward

Cars of the future could have their speed controlled by a computer, with drivers denied even the option of breaking the limit.

The Government is examining the results of research into 'intelligent speed adaptation technology' carried out by the Institute for Transport Studies at Leeds University.

The system builds on devices already well known to road users: speed-limiters, such as those already fitted on coaches and heavy lorries, and satellite positioning, as found in anti-theft trackers and in-car navigation.

By combining the two technologies, cars can be controlled remotely.

The institute installed the system on 20 cars, and programmed speed limits on to an in-car digital map.

For the first month, drivers were told of the speed limit, but were left to decide whether to observe it.

For the following four months, the car was forced to slow down as the technology took over control of the accelerator pedal.

Then, for a final month, the driver was given full control of the car again.

The purpose of the research, according to the Department of Transport, was to examine how the technology affected driver behaviour.

There are no plans to make it compulsory. For the time being, at least, transport officials have ruled out another version of the system which could use roadside beacons – already in operation for some road-charging systems – to send signals to a passing car and ensure that it remained within the speed limit.

However, companies such as Siemens are experimenting with a consumer version of the product which, it is believed, may appeal to motorists. One potential market would be the driver who has amassed a number of penalty points on his or her licence and wants to avoid disqualification.

By adding speed limit data to existing satellite navigation systems, the driver could be told of the limit and then be forced to stick to it as the flow of fuel to the accelerator was controlled.

An alternative use would be to link the speed-limiter to an anti-theft tracker. Thus it would not only be possible to locate a stolen car, but also make it impossible for the thief to take it above a pre-set speed, such as 20 mph.

In its simplest form, a driver would need only a speed-limiter and a receiver, normally a small black box similar in size to a mobile phone, capable of picking up the satellite signal.

'It just needs the box to know where you are,' said Andy Reeves, a product manager with Siemens. If the system was produced on a large scale, it could cost as little as £100, he added.

© *Telegraph Group Ltd, 22 August 2005*

Support for speed cameras

Support for speed cameras becomes increasingly fragile

Support for the use of speed cameras to enforce speed limits on UK roads has fallen below 70 per cent, the AA Motoring Trust will reveal in a speech to international road safety experts today.*

In July 2002, 76 per cent of motorists found it acceptable 'for the police to use speed cameras at the side of the road to identify vehicles involved in speeding offences'. This acceptability dropped last month to 69 per cent.**

Andrew Howard, head of road safety for the AA Motoring Trust, will tell delegates that, in Britain, laws are only successful when they have strong public acceptance. However, at least a quarter of UK households now has at least one person with a speeding conviction in it.

'At the moment, the speed camera approach risks losing public acceptance if people believe camera enforcement is not justified,' says Andrew Howard.

'On the face of it, the fact that two-thirds of UK drivers believe that speed cameras are the right way to reduce speeding on our roads should be a good sign. But, when driver confidence continues to ebb away more than 10 years after speed cameras were introduced, it shows that the authorities and road safety professionals are failing to carry popular opinion with them and convince motorists that speed camera enforcement actually benefits them.'

'Too many motorists see themselves as victims of speed cameras rather than the cameras improving their safety.'

Notes

*Andrew Howard is addressing a conference entitled International Best Practice in Road Speed Management in Birmingham. The conference draws expert speakers from the Government, local authorities, police, transport research organisations, and foreign countries, including Australia, Holland, USA and France.

** Source: NOP Automotive, commissioned by the AA Motoring Trust. Research carried out on the weekends of 24-26 June and 1-3 July 2005. Sample size – 500 motorists across mainland Britain.
21 July 2005

■ The above information is reprinted with kind permission from the AA Motoring Trust. Visit www.aatrust.com for more information.

© *The AA Motoring Trust 2006*

Driving by the seat of your pants for safety

By Roger Highfield and Nic Fleming in Dublin

Vibrating the bottoms, hands and feet of motorists could help to cut the most common type of car accident by up to 15 per cent, according to driving simulator studies.

The use of touch to alert drivers will be common within a few years, along with 'earcons' to direct their attention and soothing smells to cut road rage, the British Association's annual festival in Dublin was told by Charles Spence of Oxford University.

> *Up to a half of all road traffic accidents are due to a lack of concentration, ranging from drowsiness to distraction*

Up to a half of all road traffic accidents are due to a lack of concentration, ranging from drowsiness to distraction. Of these, front-to-rear-end collisions are the most common, accounting for a quarter of all accidents.

Although car manufacturers have ever-more-sophisticated sensors to warn of an impending accident, they are reluctant to design cars to take evasive action. 'Because of legal reasons, for fear of being sued, car companies are unwilling to put the computer in control,' said Dr Spence.

Because extensive research has highlighted how many drivers suffer an overload of visual information, which is projected to become worse as a result of satellite navigation, internet services and so on, Dr Spence is being funded by a leading Japanese car manufacturer to design multisensory alarms. 'This research represents a whole new way of thinking about the design of warning signals for car drivers,' he said.

'Drivers are not going to like loud, irritating attention-grabbing signals that quite often predict a false alarm.' However, by linking the sound of a car horn to a location, an 'auditory earcon', simulator studies that will be reported in the *Journal of Experimental Psychology* show that they encourage drivers to look towards a source of danger. 'Drivers can respond more rapidly and accurately,' he said.

Touch appears even more promising, because an audible warning can be swamped by the sound of car stereos. Tactile devices, already used in mobile telephones, are cheap, personal and pleasant, he said.

One Citroen model already vibrates the trousers of drivers to warn them when they cross a lane too slowly, which suggests that they are falling asleep. Dr Spence is extending this work by vibrating various parts of the car in contact with the driver, such as the seat belt, the seat, steering wheel and the pedals.

Simulator studies in Leeds and at the Transport Research Laboratory in Berkshire of vibrating drivers are to be published in the journal *Transport Research Methods*.

The studies show that a 200 millisecond improvement can be achieved in reaction time. It has been estimated that an improvement of driver responses of about 500ms would reduce rear-end crashes by as much as 60 per cent.

Dr Spence said the current improvements could cut front-to-rear-end collisions by between 10 and 15 per cent, adding that the Denso Corporation – the third biggest company in Japan – predicts that by 2020 all new cars will have tactile warnings as standard.

An 'alerting' odour (peppermint) could also lead to improved concentration, his team reports in the journal *Neuroscience Letters*.

Calming smells, notably lavender, could one day be used to relax stressed drivers and reduce road rage incidents, he added.

6 September 2005

© *Telegraph Group Limited 2006*

Children killed or injured on UK roads

Casualty numbers by severity of injury by country, 2003.

	Fatal	Serious	Slight	All severities
England	141	3,336	24,131	28,220
Scotland	17	414	2,220	2,039
Wales	13	179	1,537	1,729
Northern Ireland	15	156	1,299	1,058
Great Britain	171	3,929	27,888	31,988
UK (i.e. GB + NI)	186	4,085	29,187	33,046

Source: Child Accident Prevention Trust

The benefits of cleaner vehicles

Information from the Energy Saving Trust

What are the benefits of cleaner fuels and vehicles?

Whether you are a consumer, fleet professional or a business there is a range of cleaner fuels and vehicles on the market that offer significant environmental benefits and lower fuel costs.

Other benefits include:
- Reduced operating, maintenance and fuel costs
- Contribution to organisations' Corporate Social Responsibility (CSR) performance
- Reduction of organisations' environmental burden
- Contribute to national and international agreements on reducing the impact of climate change
- 24,000 deaths a year in the UK are brought on by poor air quality – cleaner vehicles are leading efforts to redress this situation.

LPG

What is LPG?
- LPG is a blend of propane and butane and it is produced either as a by-product of oil refining or from natural gas (methane) fields.
- LPG is more suitable for use in cars and light vans as opposed to heavy vehicles.
- To run on LPG, existing petrol and diesel engines need to be converted, however, diesel is more expensive to convert. New purpose-built vehicles can also be purchased from some major manufacturers.

What are the environmental benefits of using an LPG vehicle?

Emissions performance – LPG versus:			
	CO$_2$	NOx	PM
A similar petrol engine	11%	25%	-
A similar diesel engine	-15%	91%	100/95%

How much does it cost to buy and maintain an LPG vehicle?
Costs
- Additional cost for a new LPG car or van (compared to conventionally fuelled vehicles): £900 – £1,700
- Converting an existing petrol car or light van to run on LPG: £1,700 to £2,700
- Running costs – An LPG car costs approximately 30% less to run than petrol, and approximately the same as diesel.

Benefits (only for LPG vehicles/conversions on the PowerShift register)
- 100% discount from the London Congestion Charge
- Lower Personal Benefit in Kind (BIK) tax liability.

Where can I refuel an LPG vehicle?
- There are about 1,300 LPG refuelling sites across the UK. See www.est.org.uk for a refuelling map.

What else do I need to know about LPG vehicles?
- There may be a slight reduction in the amount of available boot space due to the installation of LPG tanks.
- LPG vehicles drive like a petrol vehicle and are subject to the same maintenance schedules.
- No gas-powered vehicles are currently allowed through the Channel Tunnel, although this is being reviewed.

Natural Gas

What is natural gas?
- Natural gas is mainly methane and is extracted from oil and gas fields around the world. Used mainly for cooking and heating, there is already a sophisticated network of supply pipelines in place across the UK.
- When used in vehicles, natural gas can be stored under pressure or as a liquid, hence the terms – compressed natural gas (CNG) and liquefied natural gas (LNG). Due to the weight and cost of on-board gas tanks, conversions of existing vehicles have been limited to mainly trucks, buses and larger vehicles.
- Natural gas vehicles either have a dedicated gas engine or they are dual-fuel, which means they can burn both diesel and natural gas simultaneously in the engine.

What are the environmental benefits of using a natural gas vehicle?

Emissions performance – High energy gas engine versus:			
	CO$_2$	NOx	PM
A similar petrol engine	20-30%	Roughly the same	95%
A similar diesel engine	up to 5%	75-85%	95%

Other environmental benefits
- Natural gas engines are far quieter than diesel engines making these vehicles suitable for overnight deliveries and in noise-sensitive locations.

How much does it cost to buy and maintain a natural gas vehicle?
Costs
- New natural gas heavy goods vehicles: £25,000 to £35,000 more than conventional vehicles
- New natural gas vans: Approximately £4,000 more than conventional vehicles
- Running costs: Natural gas is currently the cheapest of all the fossil-based fuels (including LPG) when fuel costs alone are considered.

Benefits (only for natural gas vehicles/conversions on the Power-Shift register)

Stevenson College Edinburgh
Bankhead Ave EDIN EH11 4DE

- 100% discount from the London Congestion Charge
- Lower Personal Benefit in Kind (BIK) tax liability.
- Vehicles over 3.5 tonnes may also quality for Reduced Pollution Certificate and a subsequent reduction of up to £500 in annual road tax. Contact the Vehicle Inspectorate for more details.

Where can I refuel a natural gas vehicle?

- At present there are few public refuelling stations for CNG and LNG, athough refuelling stations have recently opened at several motorway petrol stations. See www.est.org.uk for a refuelling map.
- For fleets, most operators have chosen to install depot-based CNG or LNG refuelling facilities. Alternatively, fleets can out-source to the natural gas suppliers, who can install, supply and operate your site on a rental basis. The Natural Gas Vehicle Association has an accreditation scheme that requires the suppliers of refuelling stations to be trained and operate to a high standard.

What else do I need to know about natural gas vehicles?

- Vehicles that run on natural gas have a slight reduction in the amount of available payload space, due to a large and, in the case of LNG, insulated tanks.
- The automotive market for natural gas is not as developed as that for LPG and fleet operators are therefore advised that contracts with vehicle suppliers ensure that sufficient support and spares are provided to minimise downtime.
- The residual values of second-hand natural gas vehicles are uncertain due to the small number in operation, but may be lower than those of conventional fuels.
- No gas-powered vehicles are currently allowed through the Channel Tunnel, although this is being reviewed.
- Legally, natural gas tanks need to be pressure tested every three years at an accredited test facility.

Biodiesel

What is biodiesel?

- Biodiesel can be produced from the oil of crops including oilseed rape, sunflowers, and soybeans, as well as from waste cooking oils.
- None of these oils should be used in engines unprocessed as they leave damaging glycerine deposits. Instead the oils are reacted with methanol to produce methyl esters – rape methyl ester, or RME is most common in the UK.
- Biodiesel is typically sold as a blend of 5% biodiesel and 95% ultra low sulphur diesel that conforms to the current diesel specification, EN 590.

What are the environmental benefits of using biodiesel?

- Because the crops used to make biodiesel take in carbon dioxide when they grow, biodiesel is considered a renewable fuel.

- Studies show that biodiesel reduces the fine particles emitted from diesel vehicles. As these particles are tiny and can penetrate deep into the lungs, biodiesel can help to improve local air quality. However, oxides of nitrogen, a smog-forming gas, are slightly higher than cleaner or ultra low sulphur diesel.
- Biodiesel is highly biodegradable and therefore does not accumulate and pollute soil and waterways.

How much does it cost to run a vehicle on biodiesel?

- Good quality biodiesel (fuel standard EN 14214) tends to cost more than regular diesel to produce. Because of this, the Government reduced the tax on biodiesel by 20 pence per litre in July 2002 to compensate for the additional costs and encourage production and use of this fuel. As a result, current biodiesel pump prices are roughly the same as standard diesel.

Where can I buy biodiesel?

- Biodiesel is available from selected petrol stations. See www.est.org.uk for a refuelling map.

What else do I need to know about biodiesel?

- When used in 5% blends with conventional 'mineral' diesel, biodiesel behaves almost identically to conventional diesel, meaning that most motor manufacturers warrant their vehicles to run on the fuel. In fact, some studies have found the lubricating properties of biodiesel can make engines run more smoothly.
- Consumers should be wary of using any fuel that does not conform to the recognised standard for biodiesel EN 14214, and meet the current diesel specification EN590, as this may compromise the warranty of their vehicle. In particular, using 100% biodiesel can create problems with engine performance.
- Most vehicle manufacturers warranty their vehicles to run on this 5% blend. If a manufacturer is unsure, consumers should check that the biodiesel they purchase conforms to the recognised quality standard for diesel fuels, EN 590.

Electric vehicles

Electric vehicles use a battery and electric motor to power the vehicle so have no emissions at the point of use and are extremely quiet.

- Due to the capacity of the battery, their range is limited (usually to 60 miles or less) between recharges and as a result they are better suited for use as city-based cars and vans with set journey patterns or a limited range.

Common uses include pool cars, delivery and courier cars, motorcycles, service vehicles in airports and sensitive areas, for example, childcare centres and hospitals.

What are the environmental benefits of electric vehicles?

- As electric vehicles are extremely quiet and have no emissions at the point of use, they are excellent for trips in towns and city centres.
- Electric vehicles produce no tail-pipe carbon dioxide emissions.

How much does it cost to buy and maintain an electric vehicle?

Costs

- New electric vehicle: Around £5,500 more than a conventional vehicle
- New electric vehicle: As little as 1 pence per mile
- Battery replacement: Around £10,000

Benefits (only for electric vehicles on the PowerShift register)

- 100% discount from the London Congestion Charge
- Electric vehicles are not subject to Vehicle Excise Duty
- Enhanced capital allowance rate of 100% in the first year
- Lower Personal Benefit in Kind (BIK) tax liability.

Where can I recharge an electric vehicle?

- Electric vehicles can be recharged by plugging them into an existing electrical socket (13 amp/single phase or 3-phase supply).
- A number of city councils are installing electric recharging points in car parks, and some are looking at on-street recharging points. See www.est.org.uk for a refuelling map.

What else do I need to know about electric vehicles?

- There is currently a limited range of electric vehicles available in the UK – check the PowerShift register for details.
- The top speed of an electric vehicle is significantly lower than an equivalent petrol or diesel car, but more than adequate for city driving and often has comparable or better acceleration.
- The propulsion system of an electric vehicle should need much less servicing and maintenance than a conventionally fuelled vehicle.
- Most existing electric vehicles tend to use a lead acid or nickel cadmium battery, although the European Commission has issued proposals to ban the use of use of cadmium in batteries for electric vehicles by the end of 2005.

Hybrid electrics

What are electric hybrid vehicles?

- Hybrid vehicles are powered by a combination of petrol and electricity.
- Current models include the Toyota Prius, Honda Insight and Honda Civic IMA. These vehicles have a petrol engine and an electric motor powered by an energy storage device such as a battery pack.
- All hybrids use regenerative braking, which means that energy is put back into the battery when braking – this improves energy efficiency and reduces brake wear.

24,000 deaths a year in the UK are brought on by poor air quality – cleaner vehicles are leading efforts to redress this situation

---

What are the environmental benefits of an electric hybrid vehicle?

- Hybrid technologies improve fuel efficiency and therefore provide considerable fuel savings compared to a normal petrol vehicle.

How much does it cost to buy and maintain an electric hybrid vehicle?

Costs

- New electric hybrid vehicle: £1,000-£3,000 more than conventional vehicles
- Running costs: Two-thirds the cost of equivalent petrol-fuelled vehicle. Hybrids are typically capable of running in excess of 55 miles per gallon of petrol (5.1 litres per 100 km).

Benefits (only for electric hybrid vehicles on the PowerShift register)

- 100% discount from the London Congestion Charge
- Reduced Vehicle Excise Duty

- Enhanced capital allowance rate of 100% in the first year
- Lower Personal Benefit in Kind (BIK) tax liability.

Where can I refuel an electric hybrid vehicle?

- At any petrol station as you will only need to fill up a hybrid with petrol since the electric batteries will then recharge while the vehicle is operation.

What else do I need to know about electric hybrid vehicles?

- Hybrids can have the same performance as that of a normal petrol vehicle although acceleration and top speed may be slightly lower.
- Since hybrid vehicles are manufacturer-supplied products rather than aftermarket conversions, they benefit from full manufacturer support and normal warranty.
- Maintenance on hybrids should be equivalent to a petrol or diesel vehicle, although the dealer will require specialist diagnostic equipment to check the battery and motor.
- With regular maintenance the battery should last the life of the car. Batteries normally have a five- to eight-year warranty.
- The Toyota and Honda hybrid vehicles use a nickel metal hydride (Ni MH) battery, so they are not affected by the proposed EU ban on the use of cadmium in vehicle batteries.

Fuel cells

What are fuel cells?

- Fuel cells are extremely efficient electro-chemical devices that use hydrogen and oxygen to produce electricity to power an electric motor.
- Fuel cells were devised in the 19th century and were used to provide on-board electrical energy and water for the Apollo spacecraft.
- Fuel cell vehicles have similar or improved performance as compared to a vehicle with an internal combustion engine and they are not as limited in range as are most battery electric vehicles.
- Fuel cell vehicles can be either 'pure' or 'hybrids'. The hybrid

design incorporates the use of a battery for peak power loading. This also enables the vehicle to use regenerative braking which can reduce fuel consumption by up to 20%.

What are the environmental benefits of fuel cells?

- When fuelled directly by pure hydrogen, fuel cell vehicles emit only heat and water vapour. As such, they are often considered to be the ideal sustainable transport solution.
- However, energy is required to produce hydrogen. Therefore, for fuel cell vehicles to be truly 'zero emission', the hydrogen they run off must be produced using a renewable energy source (for example, wind or solar).

How much does it cost to buy a fuel cell vehicle?

- Fuel cell vehicles are not yet commercially available, although most vehicle manufacturers have fuel cell programmes and many believe these vehicles will outsell other vehicle types within 15-20 years.
- Manufacturers including Ford, GM, Honda, Toyota, and Peugeot-

Citroen have already demonstrated fuel cell vehicles and the New Electric Car (Necar) range of vehicles has been developed by DaimlerChrysler, Ford and Ballard. This partnership aims to make fuel cell cars commercially available by 2010-2012.

- There are currently a number of fuel cell vehicle demonstration projects running in London, including:
  – three fuel cell buses
  – a fuel cell taxi
  – a park utility vehicle

What are the current barriers to commercial production of fuel cell vehicles?

- Fuel cell vehicles operate at the highest efficiency when fuelled by pure hydrogen, however there are two problems with this. Firstly, compressed hydrogen requires large storage tanks, which means that it is difficult to store sufficient quantities on board vehicles. However, it is likely that extremely high-pressure tanks or alternative storage methods will be introduced and will go a long way to resolving this problem. The second problem is that

there is currently no hydrogen infrastructure to support the refuelling of vehicles.

- Another option is to use hydrogen-rich liquid such as methanol or reformulated petrol. While these liquid fuels do not require as much storage space on the vehicle, they must be processed on board to obtain the hydrogen. This not only adds to the weight, cost and complexity of the vehicles, but also leads to carbon dioxide and other emissions.
- Fuel cells are currently much more expensive to produce than conventional engines. The manufacturing costs need to fall by 10-20 times to be commercially viable (http://www.hydrogen.org. au).

Notes

CO_2 = carbon dioxide
NOx = oxides of nitrogen
PM = particulate matter

- The above information is reprinted with kind permission from the Energy Saving Trust. Visit www. est.org.uk for more information.

© Energy Saving Trust

Green car labels go live

Information from the Department for Transport

From today, people buying a new car will be able to tell how environmentally friendly a vehicle is as new colour-coded labels start to appear in car showrooms.

The fuel efficiency labels – announced by Alistair Darling earlier this year – are similar to those currently displayed on fridges and other white goods. They help get a variety of information across to consumers, such as how fuel efficient a particular vehicle is, how much motorists can expect to pay in fuel bills, and whether it qualifies for a reduction in Vehicle Excise Duty.

Showrooms in Guildford are leading the way in displaying the labels, and Transport Minister Stephen Ladyman was in the area today to see the first ones on display.

Speaking from Guildford, Stephen Ladyman MP said:

'Consumers will now be in a better position to consider the environmental impacts of different cars and to make an informed decision on which one to choose.

'Motorists can make a real difference to the environment as well as to their pockets by choosing the cleanest, most fuel-efficient models. I would urge anyone thinking of buying a new car to watch out for the labels – coming to your local showroom soon.'

All major car brands in the UK have signed up to the introduction of the voluntary labelling scheme. The label is due to appear in all UK car showrooms by 1 September.
1 July 2005

- The above information is reprinted with kind permission from the Department for Transport. For more information, please visit the department's website at www.dft.gov. uk.

© Crown copyright

Green cars vs. fuel cuts

Green cars could save drivers more cash than fuel cuts

Drivers could save hundreds of pounds a year in fuel bills by choosing a greener car, according to figures released today by Friends of the Earth. The environmental campaign group has calculated that motorists could save more money by choosing a more fuel-efficient car than they would from a 10p cut in fuel duty (if petrol reaches £1 a litre). It is urging the Chancellor to resist calls to cut fuel duty and to do more to encourage motorists to drive fuel-efficient vehicles.

Using Government data, Friends of the Earth has calculated the cost of fuel needed to drive a car 12,000 miles a year and has found that:

- For drivers wanting a smaller car, buying a Citroen C2 rather than a Ford Fiesta could result in a fuel cost saving of up to £460 a year, or almost £40 a month. Cutting fuel tax to reduce prices from £1 per litre to 90p per litre would save the Fiesta driver around £125 a year.
- For drivers wanting a family car, buying a Toyota Prius rather than a Ford Mondeo could result in a fuel cost saving of over £630 a year, or over £50 a month. Cutting fuel tax to reduce prices from £1 per litre to 90p per litre would save the Mondeo driver around £145 a year.
- Even gas-guzzling 4x4 drivers have a choice. Buying a Toyota RAV 4 rather than a Land Rover Discovery could result in a fuel cost saving of over £1,500 a year, or over £120 a month. Cutting fuel tax to reduce prices from £1 per litre to 90p per litre would save the Land Rover driver around £290 a year.

Friends of the Earth is calling on the Chancellor of the Exchequer to give drivers greater incentives to buy greener cars, by announcing in November's Pre-Budget statement. The campaign group wants him to cut Vehicle Excise Duty (VED, or car tax) on the most fuel-efficient cars to

Friends of the Earth

zero, to take immediate effect, phase in substantial increases in VED on gas-guzzlers, rising from the current maximum of £165 to £800 a year by 2008.

Friends of the Earth's Senior Transport Campaigner Tony Bosworth said:

'Buying a fuel-efficient green car instead of a gas-guzzler could save drivers hundreds of pounds a year in fuel bills. The Chancellor should encourage more drivers to buy greener cars by putting up car tax on gas-guzzlers and cutting it for the most fuel-efficient models. Cutting fuel tax won't help tackle climate change, but greater incentives to use greener cars will.

'The Government must also invest more, particularly in rural areas, to provide real alternatives to having to use a car. It should also look at other measures such as council tax rebates for those hardest hit by fuel price rises, such as people in rural areas on

low incomes. Cutting fuel tax might keep the motoring lobby happy, but it will make the Government's failing climate change strategy even worse.'

Earlier this week analysis by Friends of the Earth showed that UK emissions of carbon dioxide, the main gas causing climate change, grew by 2.5% in the first half of 2005. This means that the UK looks set to breach its emissions reduction target under the Kyoto Protocol. Transport is a major source of carbon dioxide emissions in the UK, accounting for 23% of total emissions. Transport emissions are forecast to rise significantly over the next decade.

Friends of the Earth is campaigning for a new law obliging the government to make year-on-year reductions in UK carbon dioxide emissions. A strategy to tackle vehicle emissions must be part of this. More information: www.thebigask. com.

7 September 2005

- The above information is reprinted with kind permission from Friends of the Earth. For more information, please visit www.foe. co.uk.

© Friends of the Earth

Alternatives to the car

Information from Global Action Plan

Public transport

Overall, public transport uses less than half as much fuel per passenger than a private car. If more people took public transport traffic congestion would quickly disappear. For example, a double track urban railway moves 30,000 people an hour. An equivalent road has 3000-6000 drivers on it.

Using public transport can be tricky but when it works it can be cheaper and more relaxing than taking a car.

Cycling is particularly good for relaxation and helping you to relax and build your fitness – this can leave you less than half as likely to suffer a heart attack

Rail timetables and fares
www.nationalrail.co.uk
08457 48 49 50
Coach travel
www.nationalexpress.co.uk
08705 80 80 80
National Travel Line
www.pti.org.uk
0870 6082608
London Travel Information
www.journeyplanner.tfl.gov.uk
020 7222 1234.

Cycling

Cycling is particularly good for relaxation and helping you to relax and build your fitness – this can leave you less than half as likely to suffer a heart attack.

You may find that cycling to work is the quickest and cheapest way of getting to work, especially in big cities like London. Many companies are now introducing cycle sheds (and showers!) into the workplace. Find out what's happening at your workplace.

For details on the National Cycle Network contact Sustrans.

The Cycling Tourist Club has information on cycling routes and estimated travel times.

Walking

Walking is great exercise, free, and the most environmentally friendly way to travel. For short journeys, walking is the ideal mode of travel. If everyone walked to work just one day a week, we could cut traffic congestion massively.

During term time 20% of traffic in the rush hour is related to children being driven to school. In 1995/97 49% of children aged 5-15 walked to school compared to 59% in 1985/86. If you have kids and you don't live too far from their school, try walking (providing it is safe to do so), even if it's only one day a week.

The pedestrian association campaigns for liveable streets not dominated by road traffic: visit www.livingstreets.org.uk. Your local authority will be able to help with school travel plans.

■ The above information is reprinted with kind permission from Global Action Plan. Visit www. globalactionplan.org.uk for more information.

© Global Action Plan

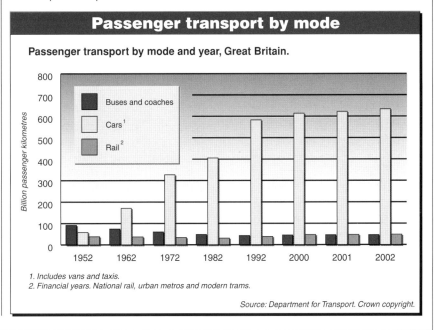

Passenger transport by mode

Passenger transport by mode and year, Great Britain.

Buses and coaches · Cars[1] · Rail[2]

Billion passenger kilometres (axis 0–800)

Years: 1952, 1962, 1972, 1982, 1992, 2000, 2001, 2002

1. Includes vans and taxis.
2. Financial years. National rail, urban metros and modern trams.

Source: Department for Transport. Crown copyright.

The walking bus

A safe way for children to walk to school

Introduction

Turn up at any primary school at around 8.40 am on a weekday, and you're likely to be confronted by a chaotic scene as parents and children make the daily dash to school. In those 15 minutes at the start and end of the school day, the school vicinity becomes jammed with cars vying for parking space. Cars will be parked on kerbs and road corners. Latecomers block school gates, bus stops, driveways and laybys. Car doors swing dangerously open on to the road, putting both children and unsuspecting cyclists at risk.

And there's nothing to suggest the problem is getting any better – in fact traffic congestion around schools seems to be getting worse; today, nearly twice as many children arrive at school by car than 10 years ago.

> **Put simply, the walking bus is a line of children, walking in pairs to school along a set route with an adult 'driver' at the front and 'conductor' at the back**

Along with this increase in traffic congestion, comes noise and pollution. Asthma, a condition known to be linked to air pollution, is on the increase. The incidence of asthma and wheezing in young children has almost doubled in less than a decade; today, one in seven children suffer from asthma.

A question of safety

Everyone with a child of school age will know that safety is the number one consideration when it comes to finding a way for them to get to school and back each day.

Increasingly busy roads make crossing them much more difficult and cycling on them potentially fatal. As it is, one child in 15 is injured in a road accident before his or her 16th birthday. Little wonder then that parents choose to take their children to school by car. Yet it's all part of the same problem.

The great news is that there is an excellent way for children to get to school safely without parents escorting them and without using the car. It improves children's health and also saves their parents time and reduces traffic congestion and pollution around school gates. It's the walking bus.

What is a walking bus?

The walking bus concept is catching on fast. In the UK, the first walking bus was set up in St Albans, Hertfordshire, in 1995 and proved to be a safe, healthy and enjoyable way for children to walk to school. It also reduced traffic congestion and saved time for parents

Simple solutions to big problems

Put simply, the walking bus is a line of children, walking in pairs to school along a set route with an adult 'driver' at the front and 'conductor' at the back. There's nothing new about parents walking each other's children to school, but the walking bus creates a more formal system which allows volunteers to walk larger numbers of children to school. Like a bus there are scheduled bus stops where children are picked up at specific times. So, like a bus, you can miss it. But the similarities end there – unlike a bus it is free, healthy and totally non-polluting. Everybody gains with a walking bus.

'I first heard about the walking bus in a letter sent to me by Maidenhead Friends of the Earth. I thought this scheme was an excellent way of reducing congestion around our school gates, while enabling children to walk to school in safety and improve their road sense at the same time. Several meetings later, the walking bus scheme was set up and has now been running successfully for well over a year.

'Our school was featured in the local press and we had coverage on Meridian Television. As a result I have had a number of phone calls from other teachers enquiring about setting up a similar scheme for their school – all good news for reducing the severe congestion schools increasingly suffer from.' Peter Brooks, Headteacher, Courthouse Junior School

The walking bus is safe

Not only do children get to walk to school in a safe environment, they also learn good road sense. Better traffic awareness gives kids more independence.

■ The above information is taken from the Friends of the Earth document *The walking bus* and is reprinted with permission. For more information or to view the full document, visit www.foe.org.uk.

© Friends of the Earth

Walking to school

It's official: children who walk to school are more active when they get there

New research from the Centre for Transport Studies at University College London shows that children who walk are more active in general. Children who are driven to school, clubs and outings are less active when they get there than children who walk.

The research, which tracked 200 children using electronic monitors and diaries to see how active they were throughout each day, shows that walking is the link between lifestyle and physical fitness. Not only is it good activity in itself – it is the key to greater activity throughout the day.

Professor Roger Mackett, who led the research, will be explaining the findings to over 130 local authority officers and school representatives at this year's Walk to School Workshop. The event is hosted by Living Streets in partnership with Birmingham City Council and takes place on Thursday 24 February 2005.

Professor Roger Mackett, who led the research, said, 'We found that walking to school can provide as much exercise as PE or games'

Professor Roger Mackett said, 'We found that walking to school can provide as much exercise as PE or games.

'And the trend away from unstructured play in the street and between friends' houses, to organised classes and clubs, has led to less walking and general activity. Even sports clubs don't give children as much physical activity as old-fashioned play'.

Jo Pike, National Walk to School Campaign Coordinator, said, 'Roger Mackett's research proves the need

to get our children out of the car to walk, and out of the house to play – as much as possible – to combat the soaring levels of childhood obesity'.

Gina Southey, a teacher at Norton Primary School, Birmingham, who will also be addressing the workshop said, 'Not only is walking to school a fantastic way for children to get more exercise, it really does make children more receptive to learning.'

The research showed that children are least active when they are at home. Giving children an active lifestyle means they are more likely to remain active throughout their life, and less likely to suffer from chronic diseases as adults.

By Hester Brown, Press and Parliamentary Officer

■ The above information is reprinted with kind permission from Living

Streets. For more information, please visit their website at www. livingstreets.org.uk.

© *Living Streets*

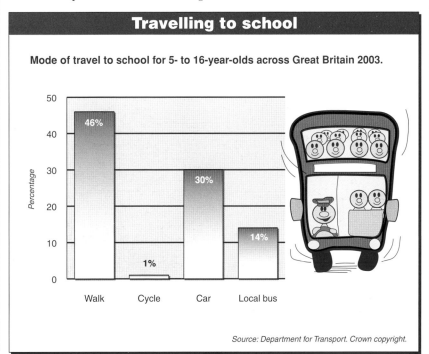

Travelling to school

Mode of travel to school for 5- to 16-year-olds across Great Britain 2003.

Walk: 46%
Cycle: 1%
Car: 30%
Local bus: 14%

Source: Department for Transport. Crown copyright.

Let's do more to encourage child cycling, says NCB

Information from the National Children's Bureau

Cycling has an important part to play in improving children's health and reducing obesity – but fears over safety mean that child cycling rates are declining, according to a report published by NCB.

Road danger and fear of crime have led to a dramatic fall in the distances cycled by under-16s, which over the past 20 or so years have reduced by 40 per cent for boys and 50 per cent for girls

Cycling and Children and Young People: A policy review by Tim Gill looks at the evidence surrounding child cycling, suggesting that road danger and fear of crime have led to a dramatic fall in the distances cycled by under-16s, which over the past 20 or so years have reduced by 40 per cent for boys and 50 per cent for girls.

The report argues that in fact cycling is a comparatively safe mode of travel, and that, mile per mile, child cyclists are about as safe as adults. It makes the case for introducing active measures to encourage children to cycle, including making the built environment more child and cycle friendly, promoting cycling for fun and as a sport, and promoting cycling for girls.

'We know that cycling is popular with many children and young people,' said Simon Blake, acting director of children's development, who commissioned the review as part of NCB's work on promoting safe and positive environments for children and young people. 'We also know that it is good for their health – not only because it is a great form of exercise but because it is fun, and encourages them to be independent and adventurous.

'That is why we need to take action by promoting public policy initiatives which will halt the cycling decline.'

As an appendix, *Cycling and Children and Young People* includes a discussion on the case for cycling helmets. It concludes that while further investigation is needed into their effectiveness in reducing injury, most adults will have strong concerns about safety and accident prevention

which will make them encourage the wearing of helmets.

Notes

In 2000 there were 25 cycling fatalities of children under 16, compared with 107 child pedestrian fatalities and 219 child road fatalities overall. These statistics equate to 2 child cycling fatalities per year per million population, compared to 13 child pedestrian fatalities per year per million population. (Child accident statistics, RoSPA, 2002. For further details see www.rospa. com/factsheets/childaccidents.pdf). *7 December 2005*

■ Information from the National Children's Bureau. Visit www.ncb. org.uk for more.

© NCB

Travel to school

Facts and figures to support school travel initiatives

Introduction

The following statistics, unless otherwise indicated in the references, were obtained from *Transport Trends 2003* and *2004*, and *National Travel Survey 2003*. You can see these publications on the Department for Transport (DfT) website: www.dft.gov.uk/transtat or order a copy tel: 020 7944 3098.

The journeys we make

Road traffic is growing

- Total traffic, measured in vehicle kilometres, is forecast to grow by 22% between 2000 and 2010.
- Overall motoring costs have remained stable over the past 20 years. In contrast, in 2003 bus and coach fares were 34% higher and rail fares 36% higher than in 1980.

We are travelling more

- The average number of journeys made in 2003 was 990 per person per year, a decrease of 3% since 1985/86.
- Average journey length has increased from 5.2 miles in 1985/86 to 6.9 in 2003.
- On average GB residents travelled 6,833 miles each year in 2003, compared to 5,317 miles during 1985/86.
- While the average time people spend travelling has hardly changed, at around one hour per day, increased car use has allowed them to travel further in the same time.

Yet most journeys are fairly short

- 68% of all the journeys made in 2003 were under 5 miles.
- 22% of the journeys made in 2003 were less than 1 mile.
- 23% of all car/van journeys in 2003 were less than 2 miles and 57% were under 5 miles.

Rural urban variation

- In rural areas 14% of GB residents do not have the availability of a car compared to 35% in metropolitan areas and 39% in the London Boroughs.

Gender variations

- Overall, 71% of adults in 2002/03 had a full car driving licence.
- In 2003 17.9 million men and 14.4 million women held driving licences.(1)
- While women make more trips than men trip lengths are generally shorter than for their male counterparts. This difference is greatest for those in their 30s and 40s, with men travelling 11,300 miles a year and women travelling 7,800 miles a year.

We are walking and cycling less

- In 2003 we made an average 245 walking trips per person per year, compared to 350 in 1985/86, a decrease of 30%.
- In 2003 we made an average 14 bicycle journeys per person per year, compared to 25 in 1985/86, a decrease of 44%.
- In 2003 we walked on average 192 miles, compared to 244 in 1985/86, a decrease of 21%.

- In 2003 we cycled on average 34 miles, compared to 44 in 1985/86, a decrease of 23%.
- On average we spend 16 minutes per walking journey.
- 39% of all households in the UK own one or more bicycles, but only 2% of all journeys are made by bicycle.(2)

We are using cars more

- In 2003 we made an average 401 trips (as car drivers) compared to 317 in 1985/86 – an increase of 26%.
- Personalised travel planning projects, which provide people with travel information suited to their journey needs, has resulted in cutting car use by 7 to 15% in urban areas.(3)

Some households have no car

- In 2002 26% of households did not have access to a car. 58% of households in the lowest income quintile did not have access to a car.(4)
- Disabled people are more likely than others to live in households without access to a car.

People want sustainable solutions

Among people surveyed:

- They support pedestrianisation policies and accept restrictions on urban travel, such as traffic calming in residential areas.
- They are in favour of road pricing if revenues raised are reinvested in transport. But they do want motorway building.(5)
- Traffic calming measures in residential areas receive majority support (69%).(6)

Travelling to school

- In general, the patterns of travel of primary (age 5-10) and secondary school (age 11-16) children are different. This is partly because of increasing independence with age, but mainly because primary school children live much closer to their schools.

School journeys are getting longer

- The average length of journeys to school has increased between 1985/86 and 2003. For children aged 5 to 10 journey length has increased from 1.1 to 1.4 miles. For children aged 11-16, average journey length has increased from 2.3 to 3.2 miles.

More children go by car and fewer walk

- The peak time for 'school run' traffic in urban areas is at 8.50am. In 1989/91 this traffic accounted for 14% of cars on the road, and had risen to 20% by 1995/1997. This has since fallen back to 18% in 2003.

Fewer children cycle

- Males aged between 11 and 17 are the most enthusiastic cyclists averaging 126 miles per person per year, compared to 38 miles (average for all ages) and 22 miles (average for 11- to 17-year-old females).

Trend for independent travel may be changing

- The proportion of primary age children travelling to school alone (with no other child or adult) has gone down from 21% in 1985/86 to 8% in 2003.
- The proportion of secondary age children travelling to school alone went down from 46% in 1985/86 to 40% in 2003.

Variations in travel and access to services

- Adults in households with two or more cars travel on average nearly four times further than those in households without access to a car and make 60% more journeys.
- Over 1.4 million people are estimated to have missed, turned down or not sought medical help because of transport problems experienced in the last year.(7)
- The Disability Discrimination Act 1995 requires that, where it is reasonable, disabled people should have equal access to transport. The DfT estimates that only around 10% of trains and 29% of buses currently meet the standards.(7)

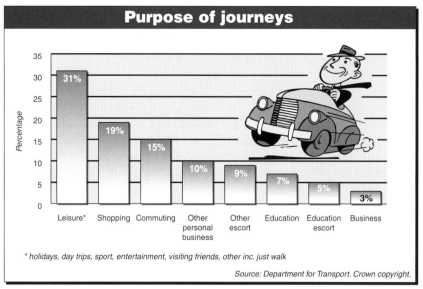

Purpose of journeys

Percentage (y-axis: 0, 5, 10, 15, 20, 25, 30, 35)

- Leisure* — 31%
- Shopping — 19%
- Commuting — 15%
- Other personal business — 10%
- Other escort — 9%
- Education — 7%
- Education escort — 5%
- Business — 3%

* holidays, day trips, sport, entertainment, visiting friends, other inc. just walk

Source: Department for Transport. Crown copyright.

Pollution and climate change

- CO_2 is the main 'greenhouse gas' associated with climate change.(8)
- By 2002 road traffic, mainly cars, was responsible for 22 per cent of total carbon dioxide (CO_2) output, 60% of carbon monoxide (CO), 48% of nitrogen oxide (NOx) emissions, 26% of particulates (PM10), and 28% of Volatile Organic Compounds (VOC).
- The majority of emissions from transport sources are from road transport, with the percentage share increasing from 81% in 1980 to 90% in 2002.
- The government has a target to reduce greenhouse gas emissions of 12.5% by 2010 below 1990 levels in line with the Kyoto Protocol and a move towards a 20% reduction in carbon dioxide emissions by 2010, based on 1990 levels.

Road casualties

Information about road casualties in a particular area can be obtained from the Road Safety Team of your local authority, which is usually located with the Highways Department.

Traffic injuries cause most child deaths

- Traffic injuries are the leading cause of death in the under 16's in the UK. In 2003, 169 children under 16 were killed and 3,891 were seriously injured in road traffic crashes.(9)
- Research exploring reasons why child pedestrian mortality rates among English children are twice those of Dutch children reveals that the reason is not that English children spend more time exposed to motor traffic than Dutch children, rather Dutch children spend half of their pedestrian time in traffic calmed/controlled areas, whereas only 10% of English children are so protected.(10)

Our child road safety record is poor

- The death rate for child pedestrians in the UK is the second highest amongst Western European countries.(11)
- The total number of child road casualties reported to the police in 2003 was 31,988.(9)
- Pedestrian death rates for children in social class V are five times higher than for those in social class I, and are higher for boys than girls.(12)

Speeding is the biggest problem

- In urban areas in 2003 58% of cars broke the 30 mph speed limit.(13)
- A pedestrian struck by a car driven at 20mph has a 95% chance of survival. If struck by a car driven at 30mph, the survival chance is 80%. For a pedestrian struck by a car driven at 40mph, the pedestrian's chances of dying rises to 90%.(14)
- Excessive speed is a contributory factor in over 1,000 deaths and over 38,000 injuries every year.
- The introduction of 20mph speed limits cuts child pedestrian accidents by 70%, child cyclist

accidents by 48% and overall accidents by 60%. There is a 6.2% reduction in accidents for each 1mph reduction in vehicle speed.(15)

Health

Car fumes are bad for us

- Car passengers in slow-moving traffic face pollution levels inside a car two to three times higher than those experienced by pedestrians.(16)
- Emissions of the most noxious air pollutants arising from road traffic should be about half present levels by 2010, largely because of improvements in vehicle technology and fuel quality. But on current projections, the trend will reverse beyond 2010 as these improvements are offset by traffic growth.(17)

- Vehicles make a significant contribution to local air pollution. The deaths of between 12,000 and 24,000 vulnerable people may be brought forward each year; and between 14,000 and 24,000 hospital admissions and readmissions may also result from poor air quality.

Asthma is on the increase

- Asthma is the most common chronic disease of childhood and it is on the increase in developed countries. One in eight children in the UK are being treated for asthma.(19)
- A Nottingham survey found that secondary school children living within 30 metres of an A or B road are twice as likely to wheeze as children living 120 metres away from a main road.(20)

Physical activity

- 30% of boys and 39% of girls do not achieve the recommended level of physical activity.(21)
- All young people should participate in physical activity of at least moderate intensity for one hour per day.(22)
- A Hertfordshire study showed that Year 8 pupils walking the school journey each day used more calories than during the 2 hours of PE they receive each week.(23)

We are getting more overweight

- About one in 20 boys (5.5%) and about one in 15 girls (7.2%) aged 2-15 in England were obese in 2002, according to the International classification. Overall, over one in five boys (21.8%) and over one in four girls (27.5%) were either overweight or obese.(24)

References

1. DfT (2004) *National Travel Survey 2003*, London: DfT
2. DETR (1999) *Cycling in Great Britain*
3. DfT (2004) *Making Smarter Choices Work*, London: DfT
4. ONS (2004) *Transport Trends*
5. Commission for Integrated Transport (2002) *Attitudes to policy options for cars in England in 2002*
6. CFIT (2002) *The Commission for Integrated Transport Report 2002: Public Attitudes to Transport in England*
7. Social Exclusion Unit (2003)
8. DfT (2004) *Transport Statistics Great Britain*, London: TSO
9. DfT (2003) *Road Casualties Great Britain 2003. Annual Report*, London: TSO
10. Bly, Dix, and Stephenson (1999) *Comparative study of European child pedestrian exposure and accidents. A research report for DETR.* London: TSO
11. DETR (2000) *Tomorrow's Road: safer for everyone*
12. 1998, *Independent Inquiry into Inequalities in Health Report*, London: TSO
13. DfT (2004) *Vehicle Speeds in Great Britain: 2003*, London: DfT
14. DfT (2005) Think Road Safety Campaign, at http://www.thinkroadsafety.gov.uk/campaigns/slowdown/slowdown.htm
15. Transport Research Laboratory (1996) *Review of the Traffic Calming Schemes in 20mph Zones*
16. ETA (1997) *Road user exposure to air pollution*
17. DfT (2000) *Ten Year Plan*, London: DfT
18. Department of Health (1998) *Committee on the Medical Effects of Air Pollution, Quantification of the effects of air pollution on health in the United Kingdom*, London: TSO
19. Asthma UK (2001) *Asthma Audit*
20. Andrea Venn (2001) Living Near a Main Road and the Risk of Wheezing Illness in Children. *American Journal of Respiratory and Critical Care Medicine*, Vol 164, pp2177-2180, Division of Respiratory Medicine, University of Nottingham.
21. Spronston, K. and Primatesta, P. (eds) (2003) *Health Survey for England 2002. Volume 1: The health of children and young people.* London: TSO
22. Health Education Authority (1998) *Young and active? Policy framework for young people and health-enhancing physical activity.* London: HEA
23. Mackett, P. (2004) Making Children Healthier Through Walking, Presentation for the Pro Walk/Pro Bike conference, held in Victoria BC, Canada, September 2004 http://www.cts.ucl.ac.uk/research/chcaruse/Mackett-Pro-bike.pdf
24. Sproston, K. and Primatesta, P. (eds) (2003) *Health Survey for England 2002. Volume 1: The health of children and young people.* London: TSO

- The above information is reprinted with kind permission from Sustrans. For more information, please visit their website at www.saferoutestoschools.org.uk

© *Sustrans*

Focus on workplace travel plans

Information from Transport 2000

Rising traffic, the most extensive congestion in Europe and an average commute time of 46 minutes... The rush hour has become the crawl hour, so what can be done to break out of the gridlock? Many employers are drawing up travel plans to combat over-dependency on cars and Transport 2000 provides help and advice on promoting car sharing, public transport, cycling and walking in a workplace environment.

Workplace travel plans offer employers a proactive approach to staff travel. Staff shuttle buses, discounted travel cards, borrow-a-bike schemes, attractive cycle parking, health walks and car share matching services all add up to a better journey to work for staff and less traffic on the roads. And recent research shows travel plans can bring about substantial reductions in the proportion of staff driving to work.

In the past five years travel plans have been gaining ground. Among councils, hospitals and colleges responding to a recent survey, the majority were either developing plans or had them in place. Local authorities are now expected to encourage all major employers to develop plans, while national planning guidance says planning applications with significant transport implications should be covered by a travel plan. But travel plans are still scarce in the private sector, and much more needs to be done to encourage wider take-up.

With traffic forecast to rise by 17 per cent over ten years, employers have a vital role to play in bringing about traffic reduction. Commuter trips add heavily to the volume of vehicles on the roads. Journeys to work make up more than a quarter of all miles driven by car or van. The proportion of commuter journeys made by driving has risen in the last ten years and is now 57 per cent.

Meanwhile the journeys themselves are getting longer with the average commuter trip now more than 8 miles. In short, we are driving more and we're driving farther.

Transport 2000's Partnerships Programme supports travel plans by researching best practice, producing 'how to' guidance and working with major employers.

Staff shuttle buses, discounted travel cards, borrow-a-bike schemes, attractive cycle parking, health walks and car share matching services all add up to a better journey to work for staff and less traffic

---

Transport 2000 has looked in detail at what travel plans can achieve and what makes them successful. The research, carried out with University College London and Adrian Davis Associates, for the Department for Transport, evaluated travel plans from 20 organisations. Their results indicated that the proportion of staff driving to work had been cut by an average of at least 18 per cent.

Travel plans successes include:
- Buckinghamshire County Council, Aylesbury
  Employees were offered half-price discount on bus fares and a third off rail travel, while walking for health was promoted. Driving to work was cut by over a fifth, from 71 to 56 per cent of staff commuter trips.
- The University of Bristol
  A car share matching service, improvements to walking and

cycling conditions and a free shuttle bus, together with a system of parking permits and charges based on individual travel needs, helped reduce the number of commuter cars arriving per 100 staff by a fifth.

- Orange in central Bristol
  Orange introduced a comprehensive travel plan when relocating staff from the edge of Bristol to the town centre. Parking was allocated according to individual travel needs, with substantial monthly payments to compensate those not granted a solo-driver parking space. The new site offers cycling facilities, a car share matching service and good access by public transport. The proportion of staff driving to work fell by two-thirds, from 79 to 27 per cent.

- Pfizer, in Sandwich, Kent
  A shuttle bus service, investment to improve public transport, a car sharing scheme and improvements for cyclists and walkers have led to a 9 per cent reduction in the number of commuter cars arriving per 100 staff. The company now offers an incentive of £2 a day (before tax) to staff commuting without a car, which has been calculated as the daily cost of maintaining a car parking space.

The Transport 2000 study found that parking restraint – for example through a parking permit system – is a hallmark of high-achieving travel plans. Other key success factors were financial incentives and disincentives to encourage sustainable travel, senior management support for the scheme and dedicated staff time to take it forward. Strategies to reduce the need to travel, such as local recruitment drives, can be very effective in cutting car use.

Transport 2000 regularly holds meetings for private sector employers implementing travel plans. The Ground Floor Partners group meets four times a year to promote best practice and exchange ideas. Participating companies hear about new developments in travel planning and national transport policy, and report on their own progress in cutting car use. Companies taking part include Halifax and Bank of Scotland, Boots, Pfizer, Vodafone, Orange and Prudential.

In the past few years tax changes have improved the position of employers offering benefits for alternative travel. But a 'parking cash out' – where commuters can choose a cash payment instead of parking – still attracts tax as a benefit in kind. Transport 2000 argues that this should change. It wants to see local authorities using their existing powers to levy a charge on workplace parking and ring fence the revenue for improvements to more sustainable travel choices, as is being considered in Nottingham, for example.

- The above information is reprinted with kind permission from Transport 2000. For more information, please visit their website at www.transport2000.org.uk.

© Transport 2000

King commute

We can't go on like this. Nothing short of a car club revolution can save us now, insists Tim Hall

You know the scenario. The traffic has been terrible, the parking worse. So the scarf is on and you are ready for a brisk, energising walk to the station instead.

But sitting there, sulking in the driveway, is the car. Well, it's pointless owning one and then not using it. And it does look like rain. So you hop in. But you will definitely take the train tomorrow.

This dilemma helps keep the car at the forefront of commuting. It's handy for those weekend trips to Ikea or to see the in-laws in the country; and once it's in the driveway it is difficult not to use it every day.

But for those who are fed up with gridlock, and are perhaps feeling a little guilty about the size of their carbon footprint, there is a third way. Britain's growing number of car clubs offer quick access to a vehicle without the tyranny of ownership.

The idea works like this. You pay a one-off membership fee. When you need a car, you book one over the telephone or internet; go to where the vehicle is parked; swipe your membership key across the windscreen; the doors unlock and you're away.

It costs around £5 an hour or £35 a day, including petrol, insurance, maintenance, breakdown cover and repairs. And with clubs negotiating free parking spaces and exemptions from congestion charging, one thing is certain: motoring like this will save you money. The AA estimates that the average private car costs its owner £2,749 a year.

Driving a similar number of miles in a car club vehicle costs an estimated £707. A car clubber is also likely to drive less, especially when commuting. Figures from Britain's biggest club, Streetcar, show that those who join up drive 70% fewer miles than the average.

But isn't it all too much hassle? Less than you might think, says Carplus, a charity set up to support car sharing.

Membership of car clubs has risen from 250 in 2000 to over 6,000 today. There are 30 clubs – all of which are listed on carplus.org.uk. And with the number set to increase, it will be easy to find a car near you.

Of course, owning a car has too much to do with private space, personal possession and status for most people to want to give it up.

But if you are finding it difficult to justify keeping that expensive piece of metal in the driveway, a car club could be part of a revolution in your commuting habits.

6 February 2006

© 2006 Guardian Newspapers Ltd

Congestion charging

Why the Environmental Transport Association has promoted congestion charging from its inception

Introduction

From its inception the ETA has believed that a congestion tax is a vital part of making our transport system work, not only for transport users but also for all people and the environment.

What is congestion?

The ETA defines congestion in towns when, for example, a vehicle cannot pass a set of traffic signals in one go and on motorways as when vehicles cannot go faster than 50mph.

Why try to reduce congestion?

Congestion is an inefficient way of allocating scarce resources. If road (or track) space is in short supply then charging reduces the demand until supply equals demand. Congestion reduces the ability to accurately judge the time taken to make a journey. Given that people rarely turn their engines off when caught in traffic, congestion increases pollution.

What is Congestion Tax?

The payment by the owner of a vehicle whilst that vehicle is causing congestion.

A charge or a tax?

There is a world of difference between a charge and a tax. It could be a charge or a tax – it depends what happens to the money. If the money is spent directly on alleviating the congestion by whatever means then it is a charge. The charge would have to be collected by the transport authority and not go near the British treasury. If the money goes to the treasury then it is a tax whatever the government says. The public is confused when the government uses

---

Congestion is limited to a few motorways and cities but it is set to grow

---

an inappropriate word like 'charges' instead of 'taxes' and we hope that it is not the government's intention to mislead deliberately. To make the point clear, a charge may be levied by the government when in other circumstances a company could levy such a charge. An example would

be school fees, health insurance or a road toll. A tax can only be levied by a government. We suspect that the nature of government proposals indicates that they are intended to be taxes and therefore they should be so called. Calling them charges would give the public the erroneous impression that they would be receiving a service for the payment. The ETA is also concerned that because government is suggesting these taxes are charges VAT may have to be applied to them. Of course, as taxes no VAT could.

When does it apply?

In most places during most of the day there is no congestion so the charge would not apply. Most motorways are free flowing for most of the day so there would be no charge. Some cities, like London, have congestion throughout the working day so they would have charging during that period. Most places if they have congestion at all have it at the peak times and charging would only occur then. People would need to be able to plan their journeys in advance so the level of charge and when it applied would have to be fixed over a set time period. Any changes would need to notified with plenty of notice.

Where does it apply?

Congestion is limited to a few motorways and cities but it is set to grow. The ETA believes that charging should apply on all roads not just motorways. However, for most roads even at peak times the charge would be zero.

Who pays?

Nearly two-thirds of congestion occurs on or within the M25. This area also has the most extreme congestion. Therefore people travelling in that area will pay most of the tax. People travelling outside that area would be far less likely to pay

Concerns over congestion

MORI interviewed a representative sample of 1,075 adults across Britain, aged 15+, between 19 and 23 May 2005. Interviews were conducted face-to-face. Participants were asked: which of the following represent your biggest concerns about the impact of road congestion?

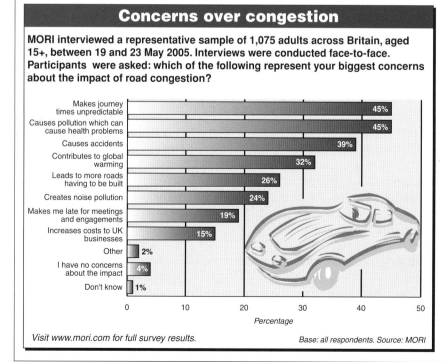

Concern	Percentage
Makes journey times unpredictable	45%
Causes pollution which can cause health problems	45%
Causes accidents	39%
Contributes to global warming	32%
Leads to more roads having to be built	26%
Creates noise pollution	24%
Makes me late for meetings and engagements	19%
Increases costs to UK businesses	15%
Other	2%
I have no concerns about the impact	4%
Don't know	1%

Visit www.mori.com for full survey results.

Base: all respondents. Source: MORI

anything. People who travel in places and at times of high congestion will pay most.

Who receives the money?

The ETA believes that the aspiration should be that congestion and therefore the charge or tax should be as low as possible. The first duty of the recipients of the tax would therefore be to lower the amount of congestion on their transport system. In our view this means that the road or track provider should receive the money.

- In the case of the European and national road network congestion the money would go to the Highways Agency.
- In the case of county ('B') roads (in Ireland, Scotland or Wales and parts of England on district roads) the money would go to the county (or district).

- Congestion money for local roads would go to the parish.

National congestion charges would be allocated, in the first instance, to improving the section of road on which they were collected. Should that stretch of road already meet the standard for a national road (segregated highway allowing 50mph average speed) the charge would be allocated to the rest of that network section (probably for rail or bus track). If the charges still exceeded the need of that section it would be paid into a national pool to reduce the charge component of the VED. The ETA recommends that county and city governments be able to collect congestion charges as they wish. Any amount they raised would be deducted from their share of the charge component of VED.

Rail congestion

Rail congestion occurs on a number of routes in Britain, but the traveller is less aware of rail congestion than road congestion. Rail congestion occurs mainly at the London rail termini, as empty trains have to be moved out of the way of incoming trains. It also occurs on the London tube system, where some routes exceed twenty to thirty full trains an hour. The pricing mechanism can be used to spread demand. Increased revenues can be used to increase the supply of services by improving signalling and removing bottlenecks at terminus stations by introducing through running.

- Information from the Environmental Transport Association. See www.eta.co.uk.

© ETA

Road charging: *the future*

Other cities 'years away from charging'. By Andrew Clark

The voice of the people of Edinburgh was greeted with gloom in Whitehall yesterday as the Scottish capital's electors effectively killed off a key plank of the government's transport strategy.

In 2000, John Prescott's 10-year transport plan envisaged that 20 urban areas would introduce tolls for drivers within a decade, pursuing a vision of smog-free, pedestrian-friendly towns and cities.

So far, only central London and a single street in Durham have done so. After yesterday's vote, even keen advocates of congestion charging admitted that other cities would be hard pushed to take the political risk.

Local authorities in Cardiff, York, Manchester, Southampton and Bristol have weighed up the possibility of charging, but all stress they are years away from a decision.

Cardiff insists its motorists will face no charge until it gets £500m from the government to improve public transport. Bristol's council was voted down when it made noises

about plans. Southampton states it is looking at the 'theory' of charging but has no immediate problem with congestion.

In private, there has been criticism of Edinburgh for setting a precedent by holding an 'unnecessary' referendum.

Economic growth, cheap cars and a desire to travel are forecast to push congestion up 20% by 2010

David Begg, chairman of the government's Commission for Integrated Transport, said: 'If Barbara Castle had held a referendum in 1968 on whether to introduce breathalysers and drink-drive laws, I think the public would have voted against.'

The setback was on the home turf of the transport secretary, Alistair Darling, who is an Edinburgh MP and a former city councillor. He has told

cities willing to consider charges that they will get more control over buses and cash from a transport innovation fund of up to £2bn.

The problem for the government is clear: traffic jams are an everyday occurrence on many of Britain's commuter routes. Economic growth, cheap cars and a desire to travel are forecast to push congestion up 20% by 2010.

Labour's green instincts oppose large-scale road building. The only alternative is managing demand by charging for road space.

Frustrated by yesterday's verdict, Mr Darling is likely to concentrate on moving towards satellite-based national road charging, which is a goal over the next decade. There could also be more pay-per-drive motorways modelled on the M6 toll around Birmingham. An adviser to Mr Darling bemoaned Edinburgh's fickle voters yesterday: 'I've lost faith in democracy. Just because the public don't like things doesn't mean they're wrong.'

23 February 2005
© *Guardian Newspapers Limited 2006*

£1.34-a-mile road charges are just five years away

By Graeme Wilson, Political Correspondent

A scheme to charge motorists up to £1.34 per mile to use the roads could be in operation within five years, it has emerged.

Transport Secretary Alistair Darling plans to have a pilot scheme covering a whole city or region as soon as possible.

He hopes a national system will be under way within a decade.

Mr Darling yesterday unveiled Labour's much-anticipated blueprint to get Britain moving.

Millions of commuters will be charged to drive on the busiest roads during rush hour.

The scheme would see 'black boxes' fitted to every one of the 31 million cars on Britain's roads.

Global positioning satellites would log each car's movements, and the information would be used to calculate a monthly bill for every motorist.

The cost of driving would vary from 2p a mile on quiet rural roads to £1.34 a mile on congested routes at peak times

The cost of driving would vary from 2p a mile on quiet rural roads to £1.34 a mile on congested routes at peak times. Someone who drives 20 miles to and from work could be charged £26.40 a day – nearly £6,500 a year.

Mr Darling claimed the radical plan could cut congestion by 40 per cent. But motoring groups raised concerns about the lack of detail on how the system would work, and said the whole thing would be unacceptable unless road tax and fuel duty bills fell.

The Transport Secretary told the Social Market Foundation in London that traffic jams would get worse as people become more prosperous and car ownership grows. While building new roads and investing in trains and buses could ease the problem, he said a long-term solution would require some sort of road pricing.

He said ministers hoped to use the global positioning satellite technology already used in many in-car navigation systems.

He admitted the scheme would raise concerns about privacy. 'For pricing to be acceptable, people will need to have trust in the system and be comfortable with the way it runs,' he said.

Mr Darling said he hoped to find a 'consensus' with the Conservatives and Liberal Democrats on the best way forward. But Tory leader Michael Howard said: 'There are lots of questions that need to be answered. Can you get a workable scheme? Will it really be revenue-neutral, or will this Government use it as another stealth tax?'

Bert Morris, director of the AA Motoring Trust, said: 'It must be seen as fair and sensible and result in less congestion.'

Paul Hodgson of the RAC called for a 'cast-iron' guarantee that fuel duties and road tax would be cut. He added: 'Who is going to pay for

The 'black box'

Serious doubts remain about how the road pricing system would work in practice. The building blocks will be the satellite tracking technology already used in dashboard navigation systems.

Each car would be fitted with a 'black box'. This would transmit signals to global positioning satellites to identify the car, the road and the time of day.

The information would be relayed to a central database to calculate how much each car should pay per mile. Motorists would then receive itemised monthly bills.

But ministers are still frustratingly vague on the details. It is not clear whether charges on upcoming roads will be flagged. Offering too much information could distract drivers and lead to accidents.

There are anxieties about Whitehall's record of botching computer projects, as well as the risk of fraud. And Mr Darling admits the scheme could be seen as an unprecedented invasion of people's privacy.

this tracking equipment to be fitted to every car – the motorist, the car manufacturer or the Government?'

Even environmentalists Joseph, of Transport 2000, said it could increase congestion on cheaper, minor roads.

He added: 'We want the mileage rate for gas guzzlers to be twice or even three times that for greener vehicles, to provide a very clear incentive for drivers to buy less polluting vehicles.'

■ This article first appeared in the *Daily Mail*, 10 June 2005.

© 2006 Associated Newspapers Ltd

Smooth-flowing traffic is on the way

As roads become more crowded, managing traffic becomes a greater priority – which is why the Highways Agency has built IT into its newest motorway

By Louise Murray

International traffic experts have been descending on a Portakabin village by the side of the M42 in Solihull to visit what is probably the smartest piece of motorway in the world.

With an 80% increase in traffic since 1980 and only 10% more capacity added in the same period, Britain's roads are becoming more crowded and heading for perpetual gridlock. In this pilot scheme near Birmingham, the Highways Agency says that active traffic management (ATM) may hold the answer.

A 17km stretch between junctions 3A and 7 is wired up with more than 500km of cabling, scrutinised by 300 cameras and spanned by over 50 plug-and-play gantries, all designed to get more cars flowing on the existing network, safely.

The idea is to use the existing motorway capacity more efficiently in two ways: firstly, by increasing the number of vehicles carried at peak times by slowing traffic (cars can drive closer together when travelling more slowly) and, secondly, by treating a normal three-lane motorway as a

four-lane motorway when required, by utilising the hard shoulder, expanding capacity by one-third.

Easing congestion

With costs for widening a motorway by one lane running at around £30m per km, and the consequent environmental and economic impacts of increased land use and disruption, the agency hopes this £6m/km pilot scheme will produce the tools to stop the entire system from grinding to a halt.

> *With an 80% increase in traffic since 1980 and only 10% more capacity added in the same period, Britain's roads are becoming more crowded and heading for perpetual gridlock*

'We chose this piece of motorway because over 120,000 vehicles a day use it, congestion is an issue, and it serves both the NEC and Birmingham airport,' says Paul Unwin, business manager of the scheme for the Highways Agency. 'ATM is a suite of technologies and we expect to apply elements at other key locations.'

Nabil Abou-Rahme, a specialist in driver behaviour working for the managing consultancy on the project, Mouchel Parkman, says: 'One of the reasons for deploying so many cameras in the pilot is to understand just how drivers are using the motorway. Motorways were built to facilitate through traffic making strategic long-distance journeys, but our automatic numberplate recognition (ANPR) cameras on every junction slip road are showing us that many drivers are local commuters.

'We started collecting data from the ANPR cameras two years ago to give us baseline data, so we can see the impact on congestion of each new phase of the project. Our information tells us we need to balance the needs of local and through traffic to bring maximum benefit to drivers by keeping the network moving.'

With 65% of congestion due to sheer volume of traffic, managing traffic flow is key, and measuring it in real time is essential to ATM. In a system called Midas, wire detector loops are embedded in the road surface every 100m. 'The loops work like upside-down metal detectors but they are a bit more sensitive, providing information on traffic volume, speed and density, and vehicle length,' says civil engineer and site supervisor Bill Stivens.

Time to educate drivers

'The Midas software then compares this with historical data for the same time of day, say 4.30pm on a Friday. If, for instance, traffic is moving 50% slower than normal, clearly there is a problem.'

The software automatically sets lane speed signs on the gantries above the road up to 2km away from any incident to start slowing traffic ahead of the queue, reducing the likelihood of secondary shunts. Many drivers are familiar with these lane speed indicators but treat them as advisory notices.

'We have much to educate drivers to obey signals,' says the Highway Agency's Paul Unwin. 'We have advisory speed limits, and from early 2006 these will be mandatory and enforced by speed cameras. The limits will be indicated by a red circle enclosing the numbers above each lane.'

Recent trials show that drivers can be quick learners, probably after painful experience. In August 2003, 50mph roadworks advisory limits in places without cameras were ignored by 90% of drivers. By February 2004, when cameras policed the limit, only 11% disobeyed the limits.

Getting the message across to recalcitrant drivers will be helped by new, large, high-resolution signs mounted on the gantries carrying appropriate pictograms, for example of a crashed car, transcending language. These can be seen from a greater distance than the older-style signs, and they are made up of over 4,000 light-emitting diodes for low energy consumption and durability.

Operators at the nearby National Traffic Control Centre control the content, monitoring any incident with CCTV cameras, and help coordinate emergency services, control lane usage and divert traffic. The whole system uses hundreds of kilometres of fibre optic cables to carry instructions to manage traffic.

The next big phase of the ATM pilot will be use of the hard shoulder as an extra lane at peak times, introducing new safety and traffic management issues that the agency and its contractors, the police and the emergency services have been working to resolve for three years. This is expected to be phased in during 2006.

Early results from the M42 pilot are very promising, says Unwin. 'We want to start on rolling out the smart motorway at key bottleneck points later this decade.'

Government targets are to reduce congestion on Britain's roads by 10% by 2010. Whether this happens may depend on how smart the roads can be made.

Background: intelligent transport systems

Applying IT to Britain's town and city roads can reduce congestion, pollution and help economic regeneration, according to the Department for Transport.

New government guidance suggests that 'intelligent transport systems' can support many policy objectives beyond those directly associated with transport, including protecting the environment and social inclusion.

Schemes such as the London congestion charge 'can deliver noticeable economic benefits through reduced journey times and increased journey time reliability, as well as improvements in safety and reduction in pollution'.

The guidance says London's congestion charging has cut congestion within the zone by 30%. On the continent, schemes to control access to city centres have reduced delays by up to 18%.

Yet intelligent transport means more than road pricing. In Southampton, parking information halved the average time motorists spend looking for a parking space. In several authorities, such as Leicester, electronic displays at bus stops are making public transport more popular. Providing drivers with more information about holdups on the road can reduce the number of accidents as well as congestion and pollution, the guidance claims.

New government guidance says London's congestion charging has cut congestion within the zone by 30%

The guidance includes a CD-ROM with a toolkit to help local authorities develop intelligent transport plans. As an incentive, the government is offering £18m to help local authorities plan road pricing and other innovations that cut congestion.

The money is the first slice of the Department for Transport's Transport Innovation Fund, which comes fully on stream from 2008. The fund will be worth £2.5bn by 2014-15, according to the department.

Transport secretary Alistair Darling is inviting bids from local authorities. 'We are looking for proposals which combine some form of demand management, such as road pricing, with better public transport, including better use of buses, tram or light rail schemes – provided they offer good value for money.'

These pilot schemes will feed into the government's wider work on national road pricing. The announcement was made on the same day that the government cancelled the procurement of a system for charging lorries by road use. This will now be 'taken forward' into the national road pricing system, Darling said.

26 October 2005
© Guardian Newspapers Limited 2006

Constraint only road to cutting car use

Information from the Commission for Integrated Transport

A new study of some of the world's leading cities has shown that the only cities to reduce car use are those that include a measure of car restraint to complement their public transport investment, a new report for the Commission for Integrated Transport showed today.

Car use still climbs in cities which have made impressive improvements to public transport but have not backed them up with initiatives to protect road space from filling up behind those who make the switch to public transport.

The study combed cities from Paris, London, Moscow, New York, Singapore, Dublin, Zurich to identify what influenced travel patterns and the measures that were the most effective.

Commission Chair Professor David Begg said: 'This study backs up the idea that both carrot and stick are needed.

'We obviously need to continue to make improvements to public transport to attract more users. But the reality is that however good public transport is, most motorists are not going to make the switch unless they have to.

'That means reduced parking spaces, higher parking charges, reduced road space (with the extra given over to buses or pedestrians) and road user charging.

'Dublin and Zurich are good examples of what happens if public transport investment is not coupled with car restraint. In Dublin bus use is up by 40% since 1996 but car use has rocketed by 28% over the same period. Zurich has some of the finest public transport but it is in exactly the same position. Public transport use has doubled in 14 years but car use is still rising by 4% a year.

'Conversely, London shows the world what can be done. Since 2000 5% of car journeys in central London have switched to buses.

'At some point people are just going to have to realise that there is a finite limit to the number of cars that any city can accommodate – and that lifestyles are going to get pretty uncomfortable along the way.'
31 March 2005

■ Information from the Commission for Integrated Transport. Visit www.cfit.gov.uk for more information.
© Crown copyright material reproduced with permission of the Controller of HMSO and the Queen's Printer for Scotland

---

Health gains from cycling

Health gains from cycling far outweigh pollution risks

The health benefits of cycling far outweigh the risks of heart attacks from polluted air, despite misreporting to the contrary, says CTC, the UK's national cyclists' organisation.

New research, sponsored by the British Heart Foundation (BHF) and publicised yesterday, has apparently shown that cyclists breathe in polluted air at higher rates than those at rest such as car drivers, and that this may increase their risk of heart attacks.

However, the study was conducted using exercise bikes indoors, and makes no attempt to compare how much pollution gets breathed in by cyclists and drivers in real-world cycling conditions. Other research shows that the air which cyclists breathe is a lot less polluted in the first place than that which accumulates inside a car. This is because cyclists are more likely to ride at the side of the road and to reach the front of stationary traffic queues, whereas vehicle occupants are more likely to be stuck behind the exhaust pipe of the vehicle in front of them.

CTC's Campaigns & Policy Manager, Roger Geffen, said: 'Polluted air affects everyone – drivers and pedestrians as well as cyclists – and is estimated to kill up to 24,000 people every year. Cycling is part of the solution to this problem, not the problem itself. It has clear overall benefits for your health, fitness and overall life expectancy, as well as helping society to reduce air pollution in the first place. We should tackling the source, not the symptoms, of this problem, and that means encouraging more people to cycle, rather than frightening them into not doing so with incorrect reporting of this important new research.'

The British Heart Foundation itself has helpfully clarified its position, contradicting earlier press reports of the new research. The BHF website states: 'For most cyclists, the benefits to their heart health from regular exercise far outweighs risk from pollution, which has yet to be directly proven.'
22 August 2005

■ The above information is reprinted with kind permission from the Cyclists' Touring Club. Please visit www.ctc.org.uk for more information.

© CTC

KEY FACTS

- Road traffic has grown by 81 per cent since 1980. (page 1)

- Over a quarter of households now have access to two or more cars, more than the proportion of households without access to a car. (page 1)

- In 2004, 53% of people felt that traffic congestion in towns and cities was a serious or very serious problem. (page 2)

- On roads with a 30 mph speed limit 53 per cent of cars exceeded that limit compared with 58 per cent in 2003; 25 per cent travelled faster than 35 mph, the same as in 2003. (page 3)

- The number of people killed on Britain's roads in 2004 was the lowest figure since records began in 1926. (page 4)

- Some 95 per cent of the 2,000 motorists surveyed by *Auto Trader* magazine said they broke the 70mph speed limit on motorways. (page 4)

- In 2003 in Great Britain, among children aged under 16 years, 74 pedestrians were killed. (page 5)

- Only one in five child cyclists wear a cycle helmet. (page 6)

- Car dependency is now at its highest level since RAC began monitoring it 17 years ago. Now nine in 10 motorists would find it very difficult to adjust their lifestyles to being without a car and admit to using their car every single day. (page 7)

- The number of private cars has more than doubled to 26 million over the course of the last 25 years with people now clocking 247 billion miles a year on the road. (page 11)

- Petrol price rises throughout 2005 left British families having to compensate for a £200 hole in their budgets across the year, says the AA Motoring Trust. (page 12)

- The 73 per cent increase in road traffic between 1980 and 2002 has resulted in a 39 per cent increase in greenhouse gas emissions from transport, which now accounts for 26 per cent of UK emissions. (page 14)

- 6,000 miles in a car produces roughly its own weight in CO_2. (page 15)

- Air pollution causes between 12,000 and 24,000 early deaths every year. (page 16)

- Support for the use of speed cameras to enforce speed limits on UK roads has fallen below 70 per cent. (page 18)

- Electric vehicles use a battery and electric motor to power the vehicle so have no emissions at the point of use and are extremely quiet. (page 21)

- Fuel cells are extremely efficient electro-chemical devices that use hydrogen and oxygen to produce electricity to power an electric motor. (page 22)

- Drivers could save hundreds of pounds a year in fuel bills by choosing a greener car, according to figures released by Friends of the Earth. (page 24)

- Overall, public transport uses less than half as much fuel per passenger than a private car. (page 25)

- The walking bus is a line of children, walking in pairs to school along a set route with an adult 'driver' at the front and 'conductor' at the back. (page 26)

- Children who are driven to school, clubs and outings are less active when they get there than children who walk. (page 27)

- 46% of 5- to 16-year-olds walk to school. 30% are driven while 14% catch the bus. (page 27)

- Cycling has an important part to play in improving children's health and reducing obesity – but fears over safety mean that child cycling rates are declining, according to a report published by NCB. (page 28)

- Total traffic, measured in vehicle kilometres, is forecast to grow by 22% between 2000 and 2010. (page 29)

- Car passengers in slow-moving traffic face pollution levels inside a car two to three times higher than those experienced by pedestrians. (page 31)

- Britain has an average commute time of 46 minutes. (page 32)

- Membership of car clubs has risen from 250 in 2000 to over 6,000 today. (page 33)

- Congestion tax is the payment by the owner of a vehicle whilst that vehicle is causing congestion. (page 34)

- The two major concerns about congestion in a MORI survey were that it would make journey times too unpredictable and that it would cause pollution which would lead to health problems. (page 34)

GLOSSARY

Benzene
A carcinogenic substance occurring naturally in crude oil.

Biodiesel
A cleaner fuel which can be produced from the oil of crops such as oilseed rape, sunflowers and soybeans, as well as waste from cooking oils.

Carbon dioxide (CO_2)
Although this is not a health-damaging gas, it is the main cause of climate change.

Carbon monoxide (CO)
CO reduces the oxygen-carrying capacity of the blood and affects the brain's ability to function correctly. In Britain, road traffic is reponsible for over 70% of CO emissions.

Commute
A person's journey to work.

Congestion
When a road is so crowded with traffic, free movement is difficult or impossible.

Congestion charge
Payment by the owner of a vehicle which is causing congestion.

Electric vehicle
Electric vehicles use a battery and electric motor to power the vehicle so have no emissions at the point of use.

Emissions
Harmful gases which are emitted when certain substances are burned to produce energy, resulting in pollution which causes health problems and climate change. Petrol used in cars is one such substance.

Fuel
A substance used to create energy for a motor vehicle to run. The most common fuel is petrol, but there are concerns that using this causes pollution, and that the cost of petrol is excessive.

Fuel cells
Extremely efficient electro-chemical devices that use hydrogen and oxygen to power an electric motor. They are not yet commercially available.

Gridlock
An extreme traffic jam affecting a number of intersecting streets and roads.

Hybrid electrics
Hybrid vehicles are powered by a combination of petrol and electricity.

Hydrocarbons (HCs)
Compounds made of hydrogen and carbon which contribute to summer smog, and can cause throat and eye irritation.

LPG
A cleaner fuel which is a blend of propane and butane. To use LPG, existing petrol engines need to be converted.

Natural gas
A cleaner fuel which is mainly methane. Natural gas vehicles either have a dedicated gas engine or are dual fuel, meaning they burn both diesel and gas simultaneously.

Nitrogen oxides (NOx)
The pollutants most strongly linked with acid rain.

Particulates
Diesel engines emit particulates (or soot) which is increasingly being linked with asthma.

Pedestrian
A person travelling on foot on a road or built-up area.

Public transport
Vehicles owned by a public body which an individual may travel on for a set fare, running along a fixed route. These can include buses, trains, trams and coaches.

Speed camera
A device installed on the roads which monitors a driver's speed to ensure that he or she is not breaking the speed limit. A vehicle exceeding the limit will have its image and registration number retained and a penalty fine will be sent to the owner.

Speed limit
A maximum speed which a motor vehicle is allowed to reach by law, varying by area.

Sulphure dioxide (SO_2)
Can cause breathing problems, affect plant growth, contribute to acid rain and damage buildings.

Traffic
A number of moving vehicles on a road or motorway.

Transport
Moving something, either people or goods, from one place to another. Methods include walking, driving, cycling or via public transport.

INDEX

ADDITIONAL RESOURCES

Other Issues *titles*

If you are interested in researching further the issues raised in *Transport Trends*, you may want to read the following titles in the **Issues** series as they contain additional relevant articles:

- Vol. 78 *Threatened Species* (ISBN 1 86168 267 0)

- Vol. 95 *The Climate Crisis* (ISBN 1 86168 303 0)

- Vol. 97 *Energy Matters* (ISBN 1 86168 305 7)

- Vol. 109 *Responsible Tourism* (ISBN 1 86168 329 4)

- Vol. 111 *The Waste Problem* (ISBN 1 86168 344 8)

For more information about these titles, visit our website at www.independence.co.uk/publicationslist

Useful *organisations*

You may find the websites of the following organisations useful for further research:

- The Child Accident Prevention Trust: www.capt.org.uk

- The Department for Transport: www.dft.gov.uk

- The Energy Saving Trust: www.est.org.uk

- The Environmental Transport Association: www.eta.co.uk

- Friends of the Earth: www.foe.co.uk

- Global Action Plan: www.globalactionplan.org.uk

- Transport 2000: www.transport2000.org.uk

ACKNOWLEDGEMENTS

The publisher is grateful for permission to reproduce the following material.

While every care has been taken to trace and acknowledge copyright, the publisher tenders its apology for any accidental infringement or where copyright has proved untraceable. The publisher would be pleased to come to a suitable arrangement in any such case with the rightful owner.

Chapter One: Our Transport Problem
Transport trends, © Crown copyright is reproduced with the permission of Her Majesty's Stationery Office, *Vehicle speeds in Great Britain 2004*, © Crown copyright is reproduced with the permission of Her Majesty's Stationery Office, *Lowest road deaths*, © Crown copyright is reproduced with the permission of Her Majesty's Stationery Office, *Majority of motorists speed*, © Adfero Ltd, *Child pedestrians*, © Child Accident Prevention Trust, *Road safety quiz*, © Child Accident Prevention Trust, *RAC report on motoring 2005*, © 2005 RAC Motoring Services, *Transport*, © YouGov, *DfT: Britain heading for gridlock*, © Adfero Ltd, *Road traffic*, © Crown copyright is reproduced with the permission of Her Majesty's Stationery Office, *Transport: frequent questions*, © Global Action Plan, *Rising petrol prices*, © The AA Motoring Trust, *The real price of petrol*, © Transport 2000, *Emissions – what goes in must come out*, © Environmental Transport Association, *Air pollution from aviation*, © NSCA, *Transport facts*, © Global Action Plan.

Chapter Two: Transport Solutions
'Invisible' speed cameras that track drivers for miles, © 2006 Associated Newspapers Ltd, *Limiting speed*, © Telegraph Group Ltd, *Support for speed cameras*, ©

The AA Motoring Trust 2006, *Driving by the seat of your pants for safety*, © Telegraph Group Ltd 2006, *The benefits of cleaner vehicles*, © Energy Saving Trust, *Green car labels go live*, © Crown copyright is reproduced with the permission of Her Majesty's Stationery Office, *Green cars vs. fuel cuts*, © Friends of the Earth, *Alternatives to the car*, © Global Action Plan, *The walking bus*, © Friends of the Earth, *Walking to school*, © Living Streets, *Let's do more to encourage child cycling, says NCB*, © NCB, *Travel to school*, © Sustrans, *Focus on workplace travel plans*, © Transport 2000, *King commute*, © 2006 Guardian Newspapers Ltd, *Congestion charging*, © Environmental Transport Association, *Road charging: the future*, © Guardian Newspapers Ltd 2006, *£1.34-a-mile road charges are just five years away*, © 2006 Associated Newspapers Ltd, *Smooth-flowing traffic is on the way*, © Guardian Newspapers Ltd 2006, *Constraint only road to cutting car use*, © Crown copyright material reproduced with the permission of the Controller of HMSO and the Queen's Printer for Scotland, *Health gains from cycling*, © Cyclists' Touring Club.

Photographs and illustrations:
Pages 1, 17, 25, 29: Simon Kneebone; pages 3, 28, 38: Angelo Madrid; pages 7, 14, 32: Don Hatcher; pages 24, 27: Bev Aisbett; page 26: Pumpkin House.

Craig Donnellan
Cambridge
April, 2006

WITHDRAWN
Stevenson College Edinburgh
Bankhead Ave EDIN EH11 4DE